WorkTopia

a down-to-earth look at work, navigating today's job market, and rising to the top

James Ferguson

WorkTopia

Copyright © 2021 by James Ferguson
Cover design by Jon Owen

All rights reserved. No part of this book may be reproduced, recorded, or copied in any form without permission from the author. Permission is not needed if quoting for book reviews or academic research with appropriate citation.

ISBN: 9798594914438 (Amazon.com)

Printed in the United States of America
by Kindle Direct Publishing, Seattle, WA

WorkTopia is sold and printed exclusively through KDP Publishing via www.Amazon.com

For permissions, booking, and interviews, email contact@worktopia.info or visit www.WorkTopia.info

DEDICATION

I dedicate this book to my amazing wife Amy, and our kids (Elijah, Levi, Hannah, and Eden) for making me feel like I can do anything and yet for always keeping me grounded. To my dad, who set a standard for "hard work" that to this day I feel like I could never attain. To my mom, for giving her all to our family through work both inside and outside the home. Special thanks to my brother-in-law, Jon Owen, for his awesome cover art.

This book is also dedicated to everyone who took a chance on me, as well as those who trained and worked alongside me. You all helped me grow as a person and professional - I have learned so much from all of you!

This book is lastly dedicated to the unapproachable supervisors who gave me no grace, co-workers who looked down on me, and everyone who generally made me feel like crap about myself at work. Without you, I wouldn't have any illustrations for my college courses and for this book. You're the best! Just kidding - but my life wouldn't be nearly as colorful without you.

"All things work together for good..."
*   - Paul of Tarsus, 57 AD*

TABLE OF CONTENTS

Introduction: In Search of WorkTopia…2
SECTION I: A Look at Work
Chapter 1: Work, Work, Work, Work, Work…8
Chapter 2: Work Daydreams and Hearing Voices…13
Chapter 3: Are You What You Wanted to Be?...18
Chapter 4: Hey Laptop, What'cha Doing This Friday?...25
Chapter 5: Slow and Steady Gets a Raise?...32
Chapter 6: Know Thyself…35
Chapter 7: Are We Done Yet? No, Never…43
Chapter 8: You Don't Know Me!...48

SECTION II: Navigating Today's Job Market
Chapter 9: Rise of the Machines…57
Chapter 10: My Corporate Ladder is Broken…65
Chapter 11: Would You Like Healthcare With That?...78
Chapter 12: Me, Myself, and Hi…83
Chapter 13: I'm Going to be a YouTuber…93
Chapter 14: It's Not You, It's Me – It's Mostly You Though…96
Chapter 15: Working From Home: "Thank You, Coronavirus!"…100
Chapter 16: Teamwork Makes the Dream Work…106

SECTION III: Rising to the Top
Chapter 17: You Can Dooo It!...115
Chapter 18: Every Person the Light Touches…117
Chapter 19: What Does a Leader Look Like?...123
Chapter 20: I Have the Power!...131
Chapter 21: Confidence…138
Chapter 22: Hey Bro, Are We Good?...142
Chapter 23: How to Get Rich QUICK!...153
Chapter 24: A Special Warning for Leaders: Triad of Danger…158
Chapter 25: What You Do, Is Not Who You Are: Conclusion…166

Introduction
In Search of WorkTopia

What image comes to mind when you see the word "WorkTopia"? Does it elicit an image of double doors opening and a unicorn handing you coffee under a double rainbow as you walk to your office? Does it sound like your work is an amusement park and around every corner there is something exciting to be experienced? Honestly, it's meant to conjure all those images because that's what we dream of as a kid – having a job that is exciting and magical. Now that you are an adult, you are probably searching for something more along the lines of money, purpose, and satisfaction in your work.

When I use the word "WorkTopia," I mean *the exact work scenario that would make you feel perfectly content and happy.* The work scenario that you are looking for might be work that is:

MEANINGFUL

CHALLENGING

FUN

Making a TON of MONEY

…and still, for some of us, our goal is to NOT WORK at all (or

as little as possible). Everyone's WorkTopia is going to look a little different. In fact, my perspective is that your WorkTopia is like going to Chipotle (or a taco bar). You might like some of this and some of that, and I might like only this and none of that. Some people like burrito bowls, while others have to have it wrapped up in a tortilla or its not "a burrito" to them. A person's order from Chipotle is very personalized to them. WorkTopia is also a very personal thing for each person. I can't tell you what it looks like for you, but I can help you get closer to it.

Regardless of what some self-help gurus want to tell you, there is no "one size fits all" approach to work fulfillment and happiness. I decided to write this book after spending time teaching business and leadership classes to Millennials and those from Generation Z at Kent State University in Ohio. My students are always hungry for practical advice for navigating the changing business world and what to expect when entering the working world – it's crazy out there! Much like finding contentment and peace in our relationships and lives, finding what you are looking for in work can be a long process. In our fast food, instant gratification world, that is a hard pill to swallow. It is much more attractive to people if you say, "follow these steps and you'll be making millions in no time!" or "buy my book, and you'll be happy with your job tomorrow!" I could say that, but I (and anyone who says that) would be lying to you. Sorry to ruin your dreams and all that, but no one can legitimately offer that to you. I *can* offer you relatable stories, encouragement about where you are, things to focus on right now, and wisdom you can use to succeed in the real world.

There is no shortage of "helpful" people out there, wanting to tell you how to live your life and offering unrelatable or trendy sounding goals. ("Do you want to have these washboard abs?!" Yes, but in the meantime, what do I do with my emotions when all I see in the mirror is a washing machine gut?) Among all the "influencers," bloggers, YouTube stars, and technological messiahs in our world…no one is talking about the *rest of us*, those who have to get up and go to work every day whether it is our dream job or not. It's not sexy. It's not, but it is where we will spend about 1/3 of our lifetime!

I'm what is called a Xennial (pronounced "Zennial"), which is a micro-generation between Gen X and the Millennials. When I was growing up in the '80s and '90s, along with Generation X and Boomers, we heard a lot more "work-isms" like "Any job worth doing, is worth doing right," "Don't be afraid of a little hard work," "Don't put off until tomorrow what you can do today," "It takes money to make money," and if you ever worked in a restaurant…"If you got time to lean, you got time to clean!".

While some young adults have heard work-isms like this, they are more familiar with and more regularly exposed to silly work memes, "the Office" quotes, and references to "Karen" customers. For work role models, young people are growing up looking at Instagram stories from people who are "Influencers" and Youtubers literally throwing around money (Hi, Mr. Beast! My kids love your channel!), along with the endless celebrity parades of people whose jobs are anomalies. (This means that those individuals who make a living via YouTube or Instagram are a unique exception, rather than a *realistic* career goal.) I want to be a voice, among the many voices and memes, that offers some real-life stories where I didn't end up becoming a millionaire, thoughts on what it's really like out there, and principles to guide you on your journey towards your own WorkTopia.

 Skip some chapters! The chapters build on one another and are grouped by topic. Each chapter is also a stand-alone commentary on that topic. Since not everyone has a super long attention span, I kept the chapters brief. Hopefully you will feel like you are knocking out chapters so fast!

 This book aims to break down essential aspects of work and make it accessible to the average person…and hopefully to give you some entertaining work-related stories about my journey. It is not an encyclopedia of all knowledge on any topic, so it will not provide you with everything you will ever need. Your professional growth is a lifelong process, so make use of great resources out there like Business Insider, LinkedIn (social media for work with lots of work-related articles), and the Harvard Business Review that add commentaries on modern business practice.

 Lastly, if I worked with you or for you, and you are

mentioned in one of my illustrations - I am not intending to shame anyone. Though, if you said something so crazy or interesting to me that I thought it would be worth mentioning in a book about work, maybe it deserves to be in here, you know? I recognize I have failed many times in my professional life, and I am very honest about that – but that's what I attribute my wisdom to. Sometimes you fall off the horse, or get hit by a semi, and then hopefully, eventually, you get up. I try to learn from my mistakes, and I hope others will too.

Section I: A Look at Work

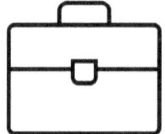

Chapter 1
Work, work, work, work, work...

"You better enjoy this summer, bud, because next year you're going to start working - this is your last summer being a kid." It was 1989, and I was 11 years old. My dad was preparing me for the real world and trying to get me mentally prepared for the years ahead when I would be mowing yards, mulching flower beds, and raking leaves for money in my neighborhood. After that, as he would say, "you are going to work the rest of your life."

That wasn't comforting to me, to say the least, but I tried to put his comment in my dad's context as a tough as nails road worker, and he always worked hard without much of a break. He was right though, it was inevitable; I was going to be working...probably until the day I died. Phew - that was a heavy and depressing thought. *But.*

I'll tell you upfront that working isn't a bad thing. It's a wonderful thing. Yes, I said wonderful! Let me explain.

Work as Part of Our Humanity

If you look at the animal kingdom, there are animals like

cats that spend their whole life sleeping or lounging, a little bit of playing, and the other half running faster than anything and viciously hunting/killing things so they can eat. It's what they do. Then there are bees, ants, and beavers that live to create, and if you move their building materials, they go immediately to building it back up. There is something inside of them that needs to build. Then there are primates that have more relational engagement, and they get regular exercise, more playing, building, and eating. They have little primitive communities that they function in. Isn't that fascinating? Where do you think humans fall on that spectrum? Some teenagers function like cats, some carpenters or engineers function like ants, and a lot of people parallel primates to a degree (other than just throwing poop and being hairy). That is not the whole truth, though; in fact, humans are very pronounced in their differences.

    Humans are designed for community, to have family and friends, to relax and play, and to have **purpose**. No other animal, regardless of their species or how close they mirror humans, has the need inside them that wants to matter and have meaning. That's what makes humans unique. All other living things function purely on nature and instinct. Humans have these too, but we have a whole other aspect that sets us apart.

    There are also no known species other than humans who have existential thinking or wrestle with their existence. In 1637, the French philosopher, and crafter of a sweet French mustache, Rene Descartes, famously made the proclamation, "I think;

therefore, I am."[1] It was a simple statement upfront, but in reality, it was deeply profound. Descartes was responding to an age-old quandary first posed by the Greek philosopher Plato 2,000 years prior![2] You may be most familiar with the modern version of this, found in movies like The Matrix and Inception, all asking the same question for the last 2,500 years: what if our reality isn't truly real, or what if we are living in some endless dream-like state? His declaration "I think; therefore, I am" was saying he cannot doubt his existence or its validity because if he can ask the question, then he exists. As humans, we are the only beings who ask the profound questions of existence like, "Who am I? How do I know life isn't just some dream? Do I matter?" The fact that you can even ask such questions proves you are unique, you exist, you matter, and life is something to embrace rather than going through the motions. No animals think this way, nor do they need meaning. We do!

A few thousand years ago, a book was written about the beginning of all things and the creation of humankind called Genesis, which is the first book of the Bible. The second chapter of this book describes the interaction between the Creator and the first person created. After creating human life, the creator took them and put them in the Garden of Eden to work in it and care for it.[3] Some of the oldest literature we have speaks about work and its intrinsic connection to our being. The idea of work should not be a negative concept for us; in fact, work is a beautiful thing! Work gives us purpose, a way to find satisfaction, exercise, mental stimulation, a venue for our creativity, and the list goes on. Work should not be seen as a way to serve corporate America; rather, it should be seen as a healthy and meaningful part of life.

Defining Work

We live in an era where many things are detached from their origin; it has been estimated that millions of people do not know that hamburgers are made from cows (hopefully most are children). So, let's at least mention the basics and definitions of work to make sure we are all on the same page.

The Oxford Dictionary definition of "work" is "physical or mental activity in order to achieve a result."[4] Work is not merely "the place you go and do a job so you can make money." Work can be anything you do at home, at an office, for school, in your flower bed, or anywhere – it is still considered work if you are not paid for it. Sometimes the most meaningful work is not a paid job, such as taking care of your baby, taking care of housework, or fixing your friend's car. If someone helps you with those exact things and they aren't a family member, you typically pay them money to do it (a babysitter, plumber, mechanic). If you expand that same principle to every other area of life, that's how the working world was built: someone specializing in specific tasks helping someone in need, for payment. Work is purposefully creating, organizing, managing, and deconstructing in any way, shape, or form. We work every day, whether it is making your bed, shopping for food, changing diapers, watching children, making dinner, managing other workers, or building a house. All of those things are work, and even though in many circumstances we get paid to work, we also work for free all the time for ourselves!

If you were working on mowing your yard and mulching your flowerbeds and wanted help - you might ask a friend to help you. Realizing what you were doing is hard work, you might offer to pay them $50 to help you for an afternoon. Whether they were helpful or not would determine how good you felt about paying them that $50. Say they ended up doing most of the work for you; it might be worth every penny…but if you end up doing all the work and they stand around talking the whole time, you might feel like *five* dollars was too much. If you expand that scenario, that is what employers go through who hire you to work in their business. They have certain expectations and things they want you to do in return for payment.

Work is a part of life. How we view it will determine many things about what our lives look like. When you were younger, you had different views on work than you have now. As we get older, our perspectives (hopefully) change, and the reality of the world slowly hits us. This transition between childhood and adulthood can be very bumpy and jarring. Put on your seatbelts – the rollercoaster is in motion.

Chapter 2
Work Daydreams and Hearing Voices

I would daydream as a kid about what kind of job I would have when I grew up. When I was younger, I would watch Arnold Schwarzenegger movies, where he looked slick, professional, yet always ready to kick someone's butt. I thought it would be the best thing ever if I could resemble him as an adult. After all, I did spend at least 10 minutes each week lifting my dad and brother's weights (about 1.5 minutes per day, lifting a few times, and then looking in the mirror saying "whew, nice work out"), and by the time I was 30 I thought my 10 minutes a week would turn into 3 hours a day, and I would have huge muscles as an adult like Arnold or Hulk Hogan. I imagined myself going to work, having the trademark Schwarzenegger haircut, wearing a suit, and riding my Ninja motorcycle to work with my slight mullet flapping in the wind. That, I thought, would look cool...and then I would think, "oh, I guess then I'd have to do some 'office-y' work the rest of the day...but then..." and I would imagine myself getting back on my Ninja and riding home with my suit on and my slight mullet flapping in the wind again. I can't think of a more "kid view" of work. You think of what you look like going in and coming home, and there's a bunch of unknown stuff in the middle there.

    I ended up spending the first few years as a teenager making about $400 per summer mowing yards and doing landscaping, and about $200 in the fall mowing and raking leaves. I also did some babysitting and light construction. As I referenced in the last chapter, my dad pushed my older brother and me pretty hard, but he was there each step of the way, showing that it was all intentional and he was trying to accomplish something greater than just mowing yards.

    Intimately connected to these memories are also the memories of him yelling at us to stop messing around, telling us to go faster ("hustle!"), and showing us how to do it right. Having my own son, I now see the slow-motion and the "what in the world are you doing?" moments *my* dad was probably observing! I now assume he was feeling a little guilty for pushing so hard, and it was then he would say, "I only push and yell because I love you, and I want you to learn how to work hard. You are going to have people working you hard your whole life and yelling at you as you get older. I want you to be able to look them in the eye while they do it and for it not to break you." I am not the fastest worker, but when I'm doing physical labor, I can still hear my dad telling me to "get moving." While waiting in the car, my wife will laugh at me when I jog back the last 30 steps after putting a shopping cart back (because somewhere in the back of my mind, I hear my dad telling me to hustle). Do you have a parent, a mentor, or your first supervisor's voice pushing you a little as you work? If that "voice" is giving good advice, then let it speak - if it is tearing you down, replace it with a positive, motivating message.

If you grew up vastly different from how I described, you might think my dad sounds really intense. Well, he was intense back then about work, but he knew something that I didn't at the ripe old age of 13, 14, 15…he knew that much of the working world is run by people who do not care about your feelings, they don't want to hear about them, and just want the job done quickly and accurately. I've had some tough and genuinely unfair bosses who have torn me down, treated me like I was less of an adult than they were, and never said a positive thing to me. While I still don't like being "barked at" by supervisors, I have been able to bear incredible pressure and stress without breaking. Mission accomplished, dad.

When I think of work, those memories are somewhere in the back of my mind and my soul. I stopped pursuing physical labor as a profession because though I can do it when necessary, I wasn't made for that type of work. I remember the moment this fully set in - I was learning all the "closing for the night" jobs at Chick-fil-A in order to become a shift manager, and this night it was my turn to shut down the back of the store and do dishes all night. I had a mild skin condition that, apparently, was enflamed by having my hands in water for several hours, along with detergent and rubber gloves providing friction. The next day my hands were all red, and large sections of the top layer of my skin had peeled off *Blech*! Not wanting anyone to see, I hid my hands in my pockets most of the shift. When I wasn't paying attention, the store owner glanced at my hands and said, "James, what happened to your hands?!" When I told him what happened and how my hands peeled after work the night before, he looked at me and said, "You are never doing that again. You successfully closed the back; now stay upfront. I appreciate your work but seriously, never do that again." It set in that maybe I'm genuinely not made to 'work with my hands,' so to speak.

  I finished up my job at Chick-fil-A when I moved to downtown Chicago for college. There, I got my first office job, and compared to the medium-sized town I grew up in, Chicago was big, serious, and intense. I got a job at the largest real estate company in town, located in the 100 story John Hancock building, and I now worked for hardline executives whose offices overlooked Lake Michigan. I went from making $6.40/hour to making $10/hour, which to me was a decent amount in 1998. At age 19, I found myself in a foreign land, and I still didn't know what people did in big office buildings, but I was about to find out.

  I wasn't riding my Ninja motorcycle to work, and I did not have hair like Arnold (thankfully). I wore khakis, a dress shirt and had to walk a mile on the downtown streets. I passed about 20 homeless people asking me for money, through a wind tunnel created between skyscrapers that would almost blow me into the road, and then had to pass by security and use a fancy digital keycard to access my elevator. Things were different than expected! It felt good, but it was intimidating.

    I will never forget meeting my first supervisor, who was the head of finance, and one of the people with the fancy (several) million-dollar view from his office. He was a short man, full suit, glasses, thinning curly hair on top, with a big pile of spreadsheets in his hand. Throwing it down, he dramatically rolls his eyes, puts his hand on his head, and says, "What a bunch of ******* ****, pardon my French. Oh, sorry, you're the new college kid. Welcome to my own personal hell. Here, grab a stack of these papers, and I'll show you what I need." And it was like that every day. The same first sentence, pardoning his French, same sized stack of papers, and just like that, my work life was never the same.

Chapter 3

Are You What You Wanted to Be?
(Why I'm not a fireman/rockstar/cartoonist)

Apparently, when I was in kindergarten, I wanted to be a fireman (I recently noticed this when my mom gave me this picture of myself). My dad worked with firefighters and police officers, so it was tangible to me but still adventurous. My longest-running occupation choices were being a cartoonist (Anyone interested in some block letters and a dog face? I got you covered!) and then being a rockstar (I still record music and play guitar when I can). Still, neither of those worked out for me, and I'm okay with that. It's not even that I tried hard to make either happen, but other things took priority as I got older. I use my artistic and musical gifts when I'm able, and that's what matters at this point.

Echoing through the years, adults have asked the same question over and over of kids: "what do you want to be when you grow up?"

Gaining Perspective: You're not a failure

When you are in grade school and younger, your answers to "what do you want to be when you grow up" tend to be things that are intrinsically interesting, epic, and stand out as adventurous. When I was growing up, there were some standard answers such as fireman, teacher, policeman, astronaut, or doctor. These days it's pretty much a universal "be a YouTuber," or if pressed for another option, it tends towards the same familiar and interesting lines of a doctor, nurse, teacher, police officer, etc. Then there are the less likely, yea, may I even say illegal or impossible aspirations, such as a ninja or princess. Some kids say what their parents do, which to them is familiar and relatable. Occasionally kids will fixate on specific careers that are unique and almost comical for their age. From kindergarten to 4th grade, my son wanted to be an FBI agent (which, to be fair, was because I told him he couldn't be batman for a living, but "maybe an FBI agent"). Ironically, being an FBI agent would probably be a fitting occupation for him. Also unique and definitely comical is my youngest daughter's aspiration of being "a unicorn," or on her more realistic days, she will say "a princess" - to which my wife says, "well if you marry the right guy..."

You likely find yourself in a less 'intrinsically interesting' career path than when you were in grade school. Chances are, you are finding yourself working or going to school for something less epic than an astronaut, or maybe you are doing what you always wanted to do, but it seems a little more mundane than you had dreamed. Why is that? Choosing a specific career path can feel and look like this for a few reasons.

First, dreams and aspirations are different than reality, by definition. As someone who has fulfilled a couple of lifelong dreams, I can promise you that the fulfilled reality feels different than the dream felt - and that's okay. Reality will rarely match our imagination. When you problem-solve in a daydream, for instance, you can generalize your answers, but reality requires actual solutions that don't always pan out the first time. It's hard to dream realistically!

What's more, even if you achieve a dream, you may not be able to continue doing it forever. This is just a reality. Very few great ideas or successful business plans are permanent. At best, you will have to adjust and refresh your business plan over the years to stay relevant. The dream is different from reality, and reality says that there will be some adjustments to your expectations along the way.

Second, achieving some careers can feel like a journey. Some career goals take longer to achieve than others; it takes time, education, and some source of money to achieve it. To become a doctor, nurse, teacher, or police officer (or "a police" as my kids have called them) it takes time, and even after you are ready to do it, you then have to prove to someone that you can do it even though you've never done it before (job interview). These processes can be discouraging and can feel never-ending. Again, though, it's just part of the process.

    Third, you may have chosen a different career because your goals as a grade-schooler were not based on who you were or what you were gifted in because those are things you naturally figure out as you get older. Besides, the vast majority of jobs are variations on a main theme, and even some jobs *have* to be specialized. You don't just become "a doctor," you become *either* a general practitioner, a specialist, or a surgeon. One does not just go to school to be an astronaut or the president, you have a career in another area, and over time you gain skills and make choices that allow for the end goal to be possible. There are plenty of jobs that we land on in our adulthood that we didn't know existed in our youth. Hey kids, do you want to be a Project Manager or an Accountant someday? You get to use Microsoft Excel every day!! Those careers become more attractive as we realize our tendency towards organization and detail instead of being jobs that appeal to our childhood imagination. We tend to choose career paths when we are young, based on what sounds exciting to us.

    What changes over the years is our exploration of our personality, seeing what we are good at doing, our gifts and talents, and dealing with the more realistic aspects of that job.

You may also realize that, though you love football, your 160 lb. body may be better suited to watch football as an adult or play in the backyard than to go head-to-head with a 350-pound linebacker trying to hit you as hard as they can. Maybe you found that, like me, you don't like seeing open wounds - let alone being the one responsible for exploring someone's "puss problem" on their leg. If you enjoy things like that, all my respect goes to you!

More times than not, your personality and gifts will determine what field you should go into or avoid - or they will determine what *department* you work in. Maybe you're not a good choice to play professional football, but you love sports statistics, so you become a sports analyst, or you can work for the Pro Football Hall of Fame in one of their departments. Maybe you have always wanted to be a nurse because you like caring for others, but you realized you are a germaphobe and would instead rather help people with their problems - so you become a professional counselor. Mental health counseling is still technically within the healthcare world, so that would still connect with your general desire. The iconic Sigmund Freud might not be who you wanted to be as a kid or even as an adult, but modern counseling is very different from the Psychology of the 1800s. Again, the *reality* of nursing might not match what you want, but the *reality* of professional counseling may be what you truly want.

Upon hearing motivational speakers talk or watching an

inspiring video, you may end up feeling a little bit like a failure if you didn't "follow your dreams" as a kid. You didn't fail! It's actually a sign of maturity that you recognized you might not be a good fit for a certain profession. As kids, we are only capable of understanding what we want to do, not necessarily what we *should* be doing. Another aspect to this is that sometimes what we love when we are younger, we grow out of and like completely different things when we are older.

Lost Perspective

Maybe you find yourself in a career choice that just isn't working for you and you realize you should maybe go back to school and do what you always wanted to do. I actually found myself in a similar position at age 35, going back to school due to some changes in my personal life. It's never too late to change careers, especially if that's what matters to you. When I was in college, I was in class with a woman who was 65 years old – she said her husband died and so she decided to go back to school and do something she always wanted to do, which was to be a professional counselor. Wow!

Some of us might have gone into our profession, assuming it was something it wasn't, or we ended up doing it via a series of events instead of by "choice." Once you get to a certain age, there is a sense of "now or never" – is it worth changing everything at this point? It depends, but if you choose "now" and change careers, you need to be willing to put in the effort and sacrifice. It would also be a perfectly legitimate choice, upon looking at your bills and your lifestyle and think "If I push through my last ten years, I can actually retire…if I start over, I'll be working until I die…eh, I'll just stay at my job, learn how to play the guitar and start a band" or whatever would make you happy to come home to after work.

On the other end of the life spectrum, you may be fairly young, working at in an entry-level job, knowing you are meant for something more, or it's your first/second job, and you don't want to be a fast food or retail "lifer" - and that's okay!

It is safe to say that wanting to change your career at any age is a common desire. Whether or not you actually go forward with it has everything to do with how much it means to you and how hard you are willing to work for it. Staying put and toughing it out is perfectly acceptable too! Whatever you decide to do with that desire, you will want to read the rest of this book for some crucial tips as you change directions or stay put!

Chapter 4
Hey Laptop, What'cha Doing This Friday?

There is a *deceiving message* in modern Western culture that says work *needs* to be fulfilling, exciting, and always pay as much as you want it to. "Hold on, James, I thought this book was about finding WorkTopia, not embracing defeat!" Discontentment in our less-than-exciting work can sometimes come from a deeply held belief that is not healthy. Open wide, because there are some big old vitamins to swallow!

There are people who love their jobs so much or their laptop that they do their work on so much that my 8-year-old would probably say, "If you love it so much, then why don't you marry it?!" That is *not* how it is for most of the billions of people on planet earth. If you're not like that and are wondering if you even "still want to be friends" after you leave your job for the day, you're not alone.

It's interesting - sometimes, after you've been working a while, you realize that you're strangely good at tearing things apart, driving big trucks, or passionate about road conditions. All of those things describe my dad's journey to WorkTopia. He fell into his career a few years out of high school, learned on the job, and retired at about 60 years old...did a couple of odd jobs...and then got a job doing the exact same thing he always did because he missed it. Over the last 40 years, I don't think I ever heard him say he liked his job, but it has always suited him. He uses things like jackhammers, dump trucks and can scare grown men into working harder. My dad's name is "Butch" for crying out loud. I'm telling you; his job just suits him. I'm sure when he was 15 though, if you told him his work future, he wouldn't have believed you. Sometimes though, when you find something you're good at, you just want to keep doing it! We don't always know what we're good at until we do it for a bit, and there are some things we are good at that we don't particularly enjoy!

It is very honorable to do a job you don't particularly love so that you can provide food and shelter for yourself and/or your family - end of story. ***Work is necessary and a way to make money; it does not need to be equivalent to your art, personal expression, identity, and fulfillment.*** If those elements are present in your job – that is an amazing bonus. For some people, though, they may realize they are really good at blowing stuff up and decide to find someone who will pay them to do it! It's not fulfilling, but if someone will pay you to do it, that's a viable option and possibly a source of satisfaction.

Fulfillment, in general, is not about how much money you make or how important you are; it's an internal satisfaction that comes from any number of things. Money and status can feel good at times, but for many people, that good feeling eventually fades. Fulfillment can be hard to pin down, and it isn't usually something you see on the surface.

Plenty of people want an *exciting* job. An "exciting" job, just like beauty, is truly in the eye of the beholder. A friend of mine works with riggers the size of houses and blows things up for his job, and he loves it – to him, that's fun and exciting. He loves the outdoors and used to be in the military, so it's perfect for him.

Studies have shown that people were more satisfied with their work in decades past than they are in recent decades. Is it possible that workers were just more **content** back then? There have been whole eras where work was never seen as something to be enjoyed. They saw it as necessary, and of course, you want to do something you like, but that was seen as a side benefit. It seems like the average person was more satisfied in their work when there were less "frills" or benefits. During long periods of peace and financial prosperity, as we have had in the U.S., people have sought more fulfillment and enjoyment in their work. It's possible that we are becoming more and more *spoiled* in our work habits. It is important to appreciate what good things you *do* have rather than what you *don't* have in your work.

It is a fairly new goal for employers to try to make their workers comfortable and happy. The focus used to be only on employees making the employer happy - not the other way around. What matters most is that we maintain a balance in our perspective when it comes to our job and what they should provide for us other than paying us to work. It's not good to expect special treatment or to expect that you will love what you do; instead, seek to find your own fulfillment in whatever you *are* doing or outside of work. This doesn't negate getting better jobs for yourself because you should always try to better your situation if you can, but contentment is a mindset.

    The same is true for your *salary*. Some jobs will pay you what you need, and some won't. Just because you made a certain amount in the past or because you have a certain degree doesn't guarantee you will make what you anticipate. Many of us have had to take pay cuts to keep food on the table - even if we are still looking for another job in the meantime. Ideally, we will be paid what we are worth, but you should see that as a privilege, not a guarantee. There are small businesses that pay very well and big businesses that will low ball you, and it can be tricky finding the right opportunity. There is this elusive idea out there that we should make more and more with each new job opportunity. Sometimes there is a trade-off, where you may receive special benefits or a title you want but make less. This is perfectly acceptable if it is worth it to you.

    Finding WorkTopia can be like searching for a lifelong romantic relationship. Have you ever met someone who wants to be in a relationship and then spent a lifetime searching for the "perfect person"? They may even turn down dates with people because they have visible flaws, but they end up alone because they could never be satisfied with real life and real relationships. I hate to break it to you, but no one is perfect, and in fact, we're all a little crazy deep down. In the end, these people may look back and think, "Maybe I should have just given that person a chance, and it could have turned into more." There are moments in our lives when it's okay to just give people/jobs a chance, even if they might seem a little flawed or imperfect, and see where it takes you. ***Opportunities are moments to consider.*** You might find love, or maybe it won't be a long-term thing, but there is no shame in trying either way. I've had at least three jobs where I took them reluctantly because they weren't what I wanted, but after getting promoted they became exactly what I needed.

    Unless you are taking that "next step" after getting a certification or an advanced degree or have a particular career goal you are trying to accomplish, waiting for the "perfect opportunity" isn't always an option. Besides, the perfect opportunity usually requires a decent amount of experience and the ability to manage the details – just like relationships.

    If you take a job at Walmart because that's the job you can get, and that's just where things are for you – you should feel proud that you are working hard to take care of yourself and/or those you love. Whether you have other future prospects or this is it, you can find fulfillment in helping customers or use your unique giftings to support those you work with. It's worth noting that you can actually work your way into a solid career at places like Walmart and McDonald's, even though it may not sound sexy to say out loud. Both of those corporations have advanced levels of management outside of the local stores that pay hundreds of thousands of dollars, and though you may need some schooling and experience, you do have options for the future even there.

As I said, there is nothing wrong with taking non-sexy opportunities that come along and just paying your bills. There are plenty of famous entertainers who do things like this. Have you ever seen a famous actor hosting a game show or starring in some low-brow action franchise that will make hundreds of millions of dollars? These are examples of someone taking a job to pay the bills, regardless of how they feel about it as a professional, while they wait for the next great thing. Sometimes for famous people, work is just work too.

President Theodore Roosevelt once said, "Comparison is the thief of joy."[5] Another word for "comparison" here would be "discontentment." **Looking at everyone else's life is the best way to make you feel bad about the good things in your life.** We all have a role in society, and our economy depends on people who do their best and serve in less flashy roles. Without the less flashy roles, none of us could function in society. We need you, your family needs you, and what you do matters. The whole idea of "essential workers" that rose out of the pandemic is such an interesting distinction. I found it interesting that jobs like being a cashier at Walgreens were considered essential, while managers at big corporate offices were not regarded as essential. Many offices have found ways to function remotely, but their positions were not essential to keep society functioning.

With all of that being said, thankfully, you can find true fulfillment and joy in things other than work. Regardless of how you feel about your job, there are many ways to find fulfillment outside of work – such as volunteering, expressing yourself through art, having a 2nd job that might not pay well, but you may enjoy it more, or doing things like coaching youth sports.

Life is more than work, and you are more important than what you "do." Finding fulfillment in life and peace in your personal life is what matters most. Maybe it's not WorkTopia that you need – maybe you need to just do a job while building your "HomeTopia."

Chapter 5
Slow and Steady Gets a Raise?
Perseverance

One big difference between someone who achieves great things and someone who lives a defeated life is the willingness to keep trying. Michael Jordan, one of the greatest basketball players in history, was cut from his high school basketball team, which he said made him try harder. He once said, "I've missed more than 9,000 shots in my career. I've lost almost 300 games. Twenty-six times I've been trusted to make the game-winning shot and missed. I've failed over and over and over again in my life. And that is why I succeed."[6] So, Michael Jordan wasn't born a superstar – his talent was developed and nurtured through hard work, pushing through the difficult moments, and never quitting. I don't know when he discovered he could fly in the air and slam dunk a basketball, but I'm sure at that point he was glad he didn't quit! It has been made clear by Michael and others that practice, learning from failure, and never giving up are keys to success.

I love the story of the Tortoise and the hare. I think of that story often. My wife would tell you that I like it because it justifies my slowness at doing the dishes and folding laundry.

That might be true, but let's not dwell on that! The moral of the story is "slow and steady wins the race," encouraging perseverance and persistence.

Now, slow and steady might not, in fact, get you a raise…but in certain aspects of life, slow and steady truly does win the race. It wouldn't be a story that is told as broadly as it is if it wasn't true - at least some of the time. If you were trying to finish a college degree or make it through advancing your career – "fast" isn't usually an option. You need perseverance. You need to keep pressing through.

We see perseverance being a virtue in areas like running marathons, learning large amounts of information, weathering a long-lasting illness, learning an instrument, and even making a marriage work. Relationships have ups and downs, and you can't always judge the value of a relationship based on how you are doing one year into it. Some relationships, aside from the initial spark, hit their "sweet spot" several years in. Running a marathon is quite painful about mid-way through, but after you receive your second wind and finish, you have a different perspective of the race. Learn to block out the noise of the world, look at your goal, and win by taking that next step.

You may be feeling like you deserve a promotion at work, like you want to quit whatever it is that you are doing, or you find yourself staring a career change in the face. While there are a million answers to your individual questions, there is sometimes one word you need to hold onto: perseverance.

The Power of Showing Up

It may not sound like much, but part of persevering at work is showing up on time, not complaining, and doing your job. Few things are consistent in life, so it's always assuring to a manager to have people you can count on. Being someone that can be counted on and someone valuable also can involve being willing to help out in ways that aren't in your job description, like helping take heavy things to the car/inside the office for a co-worker, fixing the sink/toilet if you know how, and if there's a spill then grab the mop. Now, why would you do that, you ask? It makes you someone others want to have around. Pressing through difficulty, showing up as someone valuable, and being someone others want around will end up pushing you to the top and allowing you to eventually be successful no matter where you come from or what elements are against you.

As an action point for this week at work, find a way you can go above and beyond your job description, regardless of whether your supervisor sees or not. Make perseverance and going that extra mile part of your life!

Chapter 6

Know Thyself

A Brief Look at Workstyle and Personality

Like an orchestra, each of us are a combination of personality traits, orientations, and temperaments. Do you know all of the "instruments" in your orchestra? There is an ancient Greek saying that was inscribed in the front court of the Temple of Apollo in Greece, saying "Know Thyself." The Greek philosopher Socrates echoed this sentiment at the end of his life saying, "the unexamined life is not worth living."[7] Building on this, Aristotle later echoed this sentiment when he said, "Knowing yourself is the beginning of all wisdom."[8] This ancient ideology spoke to their value for recognizing our personality, flaws, weaknesses, and strengths. We would do well to take some of this wisdom to heart. What's the point of living a whole life if you never stop to think about how you are living it?

Over the last century, some brilliant and scientifically minded people sought to help us understand ourselves. Studies have found that people and cultures tend towards certain approaches, whether it be through your leadership, your work habits, or your personality type. Many books have been written on each of the topics I will mention, and I encourage you to evaluate yourself and assess all you can so you can truly know yourself. For our purposes here, and since many of us may not want to commit the time to deep dive into our personal psychology, I will give some brief explanations for you to see what you identify with to give you a starting point to work from.

A word of understanding and caution: All of us are born into a specific culture. In each culture, there are family units, and within our family units, we are raised, trained, and grow. We also each have different personalities, which means we may not be the same as others in our family even though we come from the same genes and context. That being said, each culture in the world leans towards different perspectives, each family leans more towards certain perspectives, and each individual does as well. Of the eight perspectives I mention in this chapter, there will be some that frustrate you just thinking about it – that is because you are likely from the other orientation or another similar opposite perspective. There are genuinely no right or wrong orientations; no one orientation makes you or dooms you to be a good/bad worker, and believe it or not, people can choose to behave differently even if they have an opposite orientation. Given enough focus or stimuli, it is possible for someone's orientation to change, but more often, a person's *actions* may just change while still *maintaining their orientation* mindset. Also, for those with ultra-social consciousness about certain terms, I don't want to confuse you. This has nothing to do with *sexual* identity or orientation – these are based on our workstyles and personality types.

Task-Oriented vs. People-Oriented: This dynamic has become a pop-psychology identifier which many people use as a way to describe your workstyle, whether it be around the house or at your workplace.

Task-Oriented people tend to live their life as a series of things that need to be accomplished. They love making to-do lists (written or in their mind), and it brings them great satisfaction to check something off their list. They tend to feel content and able to relax when their work is done and have a hard time relaxing when it is not. *People-Oriented* individuals tend to focus more on those around them, and that is their priority. A people-oriented individual will have a hard time leaving for work in the morning if they are the first one out the door, as they have to pass by everyone's needs and potential connecting points to get out the door. A task-oriented person will be focused on "I need to get there on time" vs. a people-oriented person who would say, "I will leave after I help or give attention to this person in front of me." In my experience, task-oriented people are less likely to be the one who is late, and people-oriented individuals are more likely to be late due to competing priorities. People-oriented individuals are more likely to be a relaxing person to *hang-out with* and talk to because they seem fully focused on what you are saying and will act as if they have nowhere else to be. Task-oriented people often struggle with relaxing if there are "undone" tasks on their minds. Both types of people have to learn how to function in society in their own way – as with all of these topics, just because you tend towards a certain orientation does not mean you have an "excuse" for being late or being rude. As a caveat, plenty of task-oriented people are relaxed and enjoyable to hang out with, and there are plenty of people-oriented individuals who make task lists and get things done.

Time-Oriented vs. Event-Oriented: The easiest way to explain this is by giving an example of two conflicting cultural orientations. Americans are raised to be time-oriented; we see this in the way someone is considered "running late" if they are 2 minutes past the arrival date. This is not the case for those who live in India, as they are *event-oriented* and focus on the event itself: when it starts, it starts, and when it ends, it ends. My wife tells the story of waiting for trains while visiting India when she was a teenager. Her group was told the trains would arrive at a certain time, so they arrived before that time in order to catch the train. They would be waiting well past the "arrival time" – the Americans were stressing out, assuming the train wasn't coming, and the Indians were arriving late like the train, so it worked out for them. There are varying degrees of this, but you get the idea.

Event-oriented people focus on *the event* itself and less on starting and stopping times, whereas time-oriented individuals focus on the fact that *the event starts at* a certain *time*. Like many other orientations, when the two worlds collide, people on each side think the other person is totally crazy for thinking that way.

Goal-Oriented vs. Process-Oriented: Goal-oriented people are motivated by the endpoint. It drives them to work harder, and they would prefer to skip a step in the process in order to arrive at the goal. Process-oriented people, like event-oriented people, perceive things from an 'enjoy the process' perspective. Process-oriented people often insist that there is a process that needs to be followed in order for a certain end result to occur. They get frustrated when people try to skip steps in the process. A Goal-oriented individual may feel comfortable condensing a section in a meeting or a class to get to the end, whereas a process-oriented person may insist each step be covered fully. Another way this may play out would be if you are in a non-eventful phase in life, one person may see their phase in life as "not going anywhere in life," where the other person may see it as "well this is a peaceful point in life's journey."

Introvert vs. Extrovert: This is the most commonly referenced paradigm of the orientations. The key to this one is what context gives you the most energy. An introvert is energized by alone time but feels depleted of energy after being around a lot of people. An extrovert is energized by being around a lot of people, while they feel needy and depleted while being along for too long. An extrovert may really enjoy being at parties with a bunch of people they don't know, while an introvert may feel like they have run an emotional marathon at the end of the same type of party.

My wife is very social but is also introverted. For her, a nice big dose of social interaction is satisfying, but if it drags on for too long, it begins to wear on her, and her natural inclination tends to be, "I'd rather just be home, why are we still here?" Whereas I might just keep talking after you know…5 hours…and having a good time, wondering why my wife looks so tired. Being around people for extended amounts of time will eventually become draining for an introvert. Given a little alone time, they may then feel energized again to keep socializing.

When I was working in a small office, I would often be alone for multiple days and even a week (40 hours) at a time. I would come home from work grumpy after day two, feeling almost rejected (yet there was no one to reject me). It was nice to have some quiet, but after a while, it started wearing on me and almost crushing me! I did not like or understand this phenomenon, but I had to learn how to deal with it. During these weeks, I would schedule lunches with a friend of mine, and we would just talk about life. As the lunch would go on, I could feel "life" coming back into my soul. It was then that I realized I was definitely an extrovert.

It is a fact that all humans are relational beings, even if we express ourselves vastly different or need different types of stimuli. Some introverts think because they are introverts that they don't need human interaction or avoid it, and this is not healthy. They should seek *measured* levels of interaction instead of the absence of it. Another way to look at it would be to allow yourself some alone time if you need to be around a lot of people. On the other side, some extroverts think that because they are extroverts that they need to always be surrounded by people; this is also not healthy. It is important to have times of silence, solitude, and a time when you are not around a bunch of talking so, you can have some self-reflection. Even if you must have extended alone time, it can be helpful to schedule some even brief interactions to help yourself feel balanced.

Conclusion

These paradigms are not meant to "doom you" towards poor behavior ("sorry I'm late, I'm just event-oriented" or "sorry, I can't talk to you because I'm an introvert"), or to make you feel burdened by your "diagnosis" in some way. These paradigms exist to inform you of what you need to succeed and to help explain why you do what you do. These orientations can help you in managing your relationships at home and work. They may explain why you struggle to arrive on time or why you seek others out when you should maybe be working. It also may explain why you tend to like jobs where you can be alone or "just get your work done." Knowing your vulnerabilities can allow you to take care of your own needs. The better you are in tune with who you are, the better you will be at making yourself a better worker and human being. Understanding yourself will also make you a better friend, romantic partner, and parent. The people around us typically see these principles at work on a daily basis, and will appreciate your self-awareness.

Know thyself.

Chapter 7
Are We Done Yet? No, Never.
Different types of jobs for different types of people

One day just before I was going to leave work, my wife and I had the following conversation:

<u>Wife</u>: Did you get everything done today that needed to get done?

<u>Me</u>: Oh, geez, no way

<u>Wife</u>: Well, how long do you need to get everything done?

<u>Me</u>: I will never be done with my work. It never ends. I could work for a couple weeks without stopping, but more work is added each day, so I'll never be able to say I'm totally done.

<u>Wife</u>: [pause] So you aren't coming home? Aren't you going to get in trouble?

<u>Me</u>: Hon, this job is just like that. You know how you like to

check things off your list? If I had a list it would never be done because as I'm checking things off my list, new things are added.
Wife: I would hate your job, that sounds like a nightmare.
Me: Eh. It's fine. I don't mind. I'll be home in about 20 minutes.

There are many types of jobs and one way you could categorize them is in terms of what happens at the end of the day. Some jobs, once you are done with your tasks, you no longer have work to do. Some jobs, you can get caught up on tasks, but the work is never truly done because new things are constantly being added. Still, some other jobs, are like a sea of responsibility and you just do as much as you can and leave whenever you can leave –you may take calls or emails at home. All jobs have tasks you need to accomplish, but the start and stop times can vary dramatically. I'll let you test your reading comprehension and self-identify throughout this chapter which orientations listed in the last chapter fit best with which job. I hope you can see how different styles of work fit best with certain types of workers – thus, why workstyle was studied in the first place.

Retail, restaurants, and any job that is driven by someone coming into your store needing something will have an end time because you will close and lock your doors. While there are left over tasks to do, often times they are resolved by the time you leave or first thing in the morning. Office jobs and jobs where you perform physical tasks that need to be done will often be like an inbox – once you get to the bottom of the list of tasks, you are done. New items can always be added but you can either get caught up within a couple hours, days or weeks: there is an end in sight. I have worked places that you have a list of things to do a mile long such as paying invoices, entering data into a spreadsheet, answering phones, and making deposits. If you work hard enough you can clear your desk daily and walk home satisfied.

Another type of job is a management or program/project management position that manages customers, tasks, training, administrative work, and team meetings. These jobs always have a full inbox, you will never clear it, and even if you did you would have a bunch of other things to plan for coming up. If you like to walk home feeling like you have a clean slate, this type of job is not for you. These types of jobs are busy, a little chaotic, and for people who can function with details and phone calls buzzing around their head all day, and just call it a day when they need to.

Lastly, there are the CEO, President, and Vice President type positions that are never ending in a whole other way. With these jobs, you are responsible for everything, and while you might not "live at work" or be attached to your phone all night, the expectation is that you might have to, and you will just have to deal with it. These types of positions manage the heavy-lifting type of needs (such as building partnerships with organizations or deciding what to do when your business is out of money) and giving direction for their organization (what type of business do we want to be? What is our vision and plan?). The name of the game with these jobs is finding a flow that works for you and being willing to be flexible when you need to be. Andy Stanley, a large non-profit leader in Georgia, wrote a book called *Choosing to Cheat*, and the premise was brilliant.[9] Of course, the title would make you assume that is about *not* cheating and how some people choose to – but it's actually about choosing to 'cheat on' your never-ending work hours as a leader. One of the most profound things he said was that even though he has an endless workload, that he created firm boundaries around his time. Unlike many busy industry leaders, he has a firm end time on weekdays and has hard-and-fast rules about his actual days off. He takes days off. It is easy for people in positions like this to cancel a personal event to go into work, because they are "important," but what's not easy is letting the actual important things (family time and time to recharge) *be* the important things. In a completely different industry, it has been reported by other musicians that the rapper Marshall Mathers (Eminem) has a strict 8:00am – 5:00pm work schedule, including an hour lunch break. Instead of letting his art and passion rule his personal life, he treats it as a job, even though he has hundreds of millions of dollars in the bank and it's pretty much voluntary at this point. Treating your career like "a job" is not irresponsible, it is putting everything in their appropriate place.

    These are principles and guidelines we should all try to imitate on some level. You may not have the power to say "no" to your boss, but there are surely times you could, and you don't.

It is important to understand what *type* of work you can handle. Some positions will communicate this ahead of time in the interview, but they do not always do this - so it's good to ask. It is worth noting too, that your pay tends to increase based on the level of responsibility and to what degree your job "never ends." What matters is knowing what you can handle and what you want for your life. If you do work a lot of hours, I hope you will choose to cheat (on your never-ending work) once in a while and be present in your personal life.

Chapter 8
"You Don't Know Me!"
The hidden world of your co-workers

"We caught you sleeping at your desk, James", the other manager half-smiling in disbelief, "yeah, I saw it too". The way it was briefly mentioned was along the lines of, "I *caught* you", like I was trying to *get away* with it. They didn't want a response.

    Falling asleep at work is in the top few things you should never do at work. It can be grounds for immediate dismissal, and that would be justified. How would you feel if you were paying someone money to do something, and instead of working they were sleeping? Ironically, I used to work in a sales office not too long before this, and after lunch I would always hear my middle-aged boss snoring. This large, divorced dad of two was trying to keep up with his party-girl girlfriend, and he genuinely couldn't keep up. It was mildly entertaining to me and I felt bad for the guy.

    I'm going to get real here for a bit, but it's for a reason, so please just deal with it. It's important that we all understand something: the people you work with have an entire life outside of work, and you may not realize what your co-worker is going through. When I was sitting in the VP's office listening to the one-way conversation about getting caught up on sleep during company time, this was what was happening in my personal life:

1. My sleeping was involuntary. When I did "wake up" at my desk, lifting up my head, my heart would start beating fast, and I wondered how long I was out for…and if I was snoring. I was afraid to ask anyone, and I was mortified.
2. I was working a second job in the evenings, cleaning offices after my kids went to bed. I was getting an average of 4 hours of sleep and was barely able to see my wife alone in the evenings.
3. I had a 1 ½ yr old, and 3 other children under the age of 7 years old. It was crazy at home and I wasn't getting much sleep as it was.
4. In my day job, I was getting paid $15.50/hr., of which 30% went to child support, and about $200 per month went to health insurance for just two of my kids and myself, and I had 4 kids and a wife to provide for. I needed a 2nd job.
5. I was working on my master's degree so that I could get a better paying job. My wife was attempting to go to college for her bachelor's degree, because with a high school diploma she had limited employment options for her too.

6. A few years before, I had spent 8 years as a Director of my own non-profit organization, working my own schedule and overseeing about 60 people. I was very over-qualified for my day job, but I hadn't found anything equivalent, so I took what I could get.
7. My family was renting and living in a 2-bedroom townhouse with a makeshift 3rd bedroom in the basement that we were barely making work. I applied for a loan for a small house and had just got rejected with the comment from the lender, "I'm sorry, you just don't make enough money to get a house loan." My job was inherently, verifiably inadequate for my situation.
8. I was hopeless, exhausted, this was about the time I crashed my car due to exhaustion and was looking for a different 2nd job due to this. I was stretched to my max. At first, I was proud to have my current full-time job and who I worked with, but at this point I felt like the biggest loser and failure.

My new, closet sized office was so cozy and nice…but so quiet. Even with heavy metal blasting in my headphones while I worked, it was just so peaceful in there.

What was happening on occasion was that around 1:30pm at my day job I would "wake up" at my desk. That's never good. Apparently, my supervisors and a co-worker had
seen me sleeping while walking by my office a few times. It was like I was narcoleptic, uncontrollably falling asleep at

inopportune times. Judging by the music that was playing, most of the time it was for 3 seconds here, 10 seconds there, maybe a minute or three total in the worst circumstances. These are some additional scenarios where I involuntarily fell asleep during this time: while *standing up* two times, driving home from my 2nd job at 3am and wrecked my car, while my wife was talking, while reading bedtime stories to my kids all the time, and the list goes on.

    I was exhausted, my life felt out of control, and I was miserable and depressed. I was okay on the outside, but inside I was scared of what my life had become. I didn't want to fall asleep at the worst possible times and I felt like the biggest idiot, yet I felt trapped in my situation. I couldn't make any less money, my wife was already working so hard as a store manager, and we were both trying to get better jobs by getting more education. I felt so dejected. What could possibly be more de-motivating than hearing, "this job does not pay enough to take care of your family" and then to not be able to stay awake because I'm working so hard to try to remedy the situation?

    I genuinely needed help, and at that point I had a health problem and needed some sleep! After this wake-up call took responsibility for my embarrassing actions by quitting my evening job and taking a weekend job, I found ways to get more sleep, and then I later started strategically using energy drinks. Around 1pm I started getting some caffeine in my system before the drowsiness set in, or I would take a quick walk to wake my body up.

I have estimated that I have given about 1,000 public speeches in my adult life. I have spoken to small groups, in college classes of 70 students, at churches of several hundred people, conferences with hundreds of people, performances, etc. I have had people fall asleep on me many times. Every time I think the same thing, and I've taught others to view it the same: if someone is sleeping while you're doing public speaking, that just means they are really tired and don't take it personally. I don't ever lose sleep over it (pun intended). I also know this because during my period of over-exhaustion and in college, I fell asleep in those situations and I didn't want to.

Why would I say all these things in a book so people can read and judge me forever? It's because I'm human, I am weak, and I know what it feels like for no one to care or understand. You are human and you are weak. Maybe you have health or mental health problems that are embarrassing to talk about; maybe you are struggling to work multiple jobs just to keep a roof over your head; and maybe you have all kinds of issues due to domestic violence at home – we all have things, and we all have our limits.

I was working for a rather large company years ago, and my department was suddenly tasked with doing two full time positions within the same amount of time it took us to do one, for the same amount of pay. At first, they made it seem like a positive thing, but 2 months later, I was watching people break down and rush to the bathroom to cry. I heard people go off on supervisors, we had multiple people walk out and never come back, and several people referenced their increased drinking at home and arguing with their family more. It was a mess, and we were told to just keep pressing through until things evened out. Whether it is how we are treated *at* work or *outside* work, we all get to a point to where our bodies, minds, and emotions can only take so much.

As an employee, you need to expect that poor performance is going to lead to a poor reputation and possibly getting fired. If a supervisor has grace on you, it should be seen as grace and not an expectation.

If you are falling asleep, giving attitude to your supervisor, are unable to account for why you're not getting things in on time, not meeting goals, and especially if you've had to have corrective performance reviews...the writing should be on the walls for you that if you don't correct your course, you should either resign or expect to lose your job. No matter what your reasons are, that is kind of the black and white nature of job performance and job security.

As a supervisor, the other side of this coin is a whole other message. Humans are weak, we have lives, and you do not know what is happening in their lives. If someone is failing hard, you should actually talk to them. Ask them their perspective, how they feel like they are doing, and allow them to talk. It would be a tool of an exceptional manager to say things like "Anything you share with me can be confidential if needed – is there anything going on in your personal life that I should be aware of?"

Remember that one time I got in trouble for falling asleep and I realized I needed help and a life change? (two minutes ago, for you; several years, for me). Soon after that whole event, believe it or not, everyone above me either lost their jobs, quit, or retired. Within a couple months, seven people transitioned out of an office of ten people. Next thing I knew there was a new intimidating interim department vice president who was going to fill-in until we replaced the necessary positions. He was a vice president from another part of the organization, and he was the size of an NFL linebacker. He called me into his office and sat me down for a "chat." His very presence let you know that he was in charge, even if he did have a kind voice. He told me he was aware of my run-ins with the previous manager, and that he wanted to offer me a clean slate if I would commit to do my best. That sounded great to me, and after that I was his biggest fan. The four positions above me were open and I submitted my resume…and heard nothing. The positions were vacant for a couple months, and I continued to do my job the best I could. Next thing I knew *I* was losing my job because the four people above me provided my workload and I was the weakest link (see previous paragraphs).

On my exit interview, the interim department manager

asked for my keys and offered to look over my resume to help me in my job search. He was as supportive as he could be in that situation. After reading my resume, his head shot up. He was amazed at my experience, my education, and concluded that I was overqualified for the position I was vacating. I said, "yeah, that's why I gave you my resume several weeks ago." With a resigned look of clarity, he said, "Well…this wasn't the right position for you, and you are going to find something better. I'll be a reference; put me down on your resume and use my title. Here is my card." He looked me straight in the eye and said, "You didn't get fired - you quit. This wasn't a good fit for you James, I accept your resignation." I was shocked and thanked him for his kindness. He wasn't giving me the grace I *wanted* (a second chance, doing a higher paying job) – but he gave me what I really *needed* at that moment in my life: someone who believed in my ability to achieve more and to vouch for me. Honestly, that moment changed the direction of my life.

This was a very difficult time for me, but it ended up being for the best. I got a better job in a fairly prestigious company in my city and was able to do something I was more qualified for and it looked great on my resume. This new job, and my new master's degree allowed me to fulfill a longstanding dream of mine: to teach at the college level. A year and a half later in the evenings, I was standing in front of a class full of students who were ready to hear what I had to say about the business world – and I had much more to say than I used to.

Section II: Navigating Today's Job Market

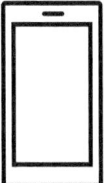

Chapter 9

The Rise of the Machines
Industrial Revolutions

We are in the middle of a revolution, but you may not have noticed. You may not have noticed it because you are *part* of this silent but visible revolution. Do you have a cell phone that is connected to the internet on you at the moment? Do you use computers to do work and save the data on them to be used later? Do you talk to your TV, phone, iPad, or car…and it talks back to you? If the answer is "yes" to any of those, you are part of a revolution.

    The first revolution was from approximately 1760 to about 1820, known as the Industrial Revolution. This was a time when the whole of Western Society began switching to new manufacturing processes. The process changed from hand-made production to machine-based, and new approaches were created to enhance the power and process of how things were made. The Second Industrial Revolution (1880 – 1950), as it is now known, was termed the Technological Revolution, having electrical power and telephones at the forefront of our life change. The Third Industrial Revolution, known as the Digital Revolution, revolves around using computers and the internet to change how we do business.

If you were alive in the 1980s and you are reading this book, you should have some connection to the analog era and the digital era. Technology started making huge steps forward in the 1980s, and in the proceeding years, technological advances began to exponentially move upwards with innovations and new inventions. I am old enough to remember using rotary phones with cords, a typewriter to write school papers, listening to a record player, having cassette tapes, VHS tapes, and filing cabinets. I used computers in grade school, but they were the kind with green and black screens, no mouse, and where you used function keys (F5) just to get around on a screen. I was a senior in high school before surfing the internet for the first time. In my freshman year of college in 1998, my college in downtown Chicago installed broadband internet for the first time throughout their campus. We still used dial-up when we were off-campus. Fast forward a couple of years; I had a cell phone and was texting, using email, and soon after that, I was creating webpages at work. I went from "I used the internet for the first time" to designing webpages for my job within six years. I've been part of several "analog to digital" transitions in offices over the last 20 years and have often been seen as "the tech guy" even when I felt like I wasn't entirely sure what I was doing. The reason for all of this is because I had to learn by necessity to operate in my cultural context. The digital revolution was progressing, and I had to adapt to survive. Things changed so rapidly when I was in my 20s that even though I had comparatively less experience than my friends, I still had more experience than those older than me.

You may not realize this, but we live in a unique era where all generations present on the earth have vastly different understandings of how to run a successful business in the world. While human interaction has changed very little, the medium by which humans interact has changed dramatically in the last 100 years. This has not always been the case! If you were born in the 1700s, the way you would run a business would not have changed dramatically between the way your great grandparent did it compared to how you would do it. So, your great-grandfather could give you business advice, and it would still be mostly relevant, though somewhat dated. If you were born in 1920, your great-grandfather would still be able to give business advice, and though it would sound dated, it would still be relevant. If you were born after 1980, the odds that your grandparent would even understand how to start a business in your cultural context would be almost useless aside from how you would treat people. What customers expect and their buying behaviors are so different from 100 years ago that the vast majority of business advice you would need to function today would not have even existed 100 years ago. That's a huge deal. This is why it's called a revolution.

For a modern, unrealistic, yet mildly entertaining and lighthearted take on this topic, see "An American Pickle" with Seth Rogan. This movie is meant to be ridiculous and to highlight significant changes in our worldviews over the last 100 years, but you can also see a Millennial and his great-grandfather both trying to start businesses in today's social landscape.

I should add that while older generations may need to adjust to modern approaches and processes, they still have a lot to offer in terms of teaching us about customer service and building customer loyalty. Unfortunately, all too often, our digital business methods lose that personal touch. We have a lot to learn from the business leaders in the past who could elicit such brand and business loyalty back in their day.

With these shifts taking place, there are whole generations who have different relationships to the technology we use every day. The age at which people are introduced to technology mostly determines their comfort with it. These categories do not include the most cutting-edge individuals of their generation but more the general attitude as a whole. We live in an era where our oldest generation was introduced to the digital age after the age of 60 years old and therefore *have a hard time engaging with it* (those part of the GI Generation and the Silent Generation). Those who were introduced to the digital age during their middle-aged years *use* it daily but have varying degrees of trust in it (Baby Boomers). Those who were introduced to the digital age in their young adult years are the ones who helped *invent it* (Generation X) along with cutting edge Boomers like Bill Gates and Steve Jobs. Those who were introduced to the digital age in their youth basically *perfected its use* (Millennials). Those who know nothing other than the digital age *don't know how to function without it* (Generation Z).

    Yes, there are exceptions to every rule – meaning, yes, I'm sure there are great-grandparents who use Twitter and Generation Z kids who can't use an iPad, but those scenarios are an anomaly for the most part. Most people over the age of 80 are not using Google as their primary source of basic information, and people under the age of 15 have grown-up in a time when the internet has always existed and is now treated as a utility - like electric and water bills.

    If you are going to be working with other humans in places of business, you are inevitably going to be exposed to or work with people all along this digital spectrum. If you are seriously lagging behind the current business trends and are refusing to embrace the digital age, you are going to be crying little floppy disc tears someday. Things are not going back. There may be a resurgence of appreciation for old technology, such as the current raging popularity of "retro style," but the world will never truly travel back in time.

    As the youngest of Generation X or the oldest of the Millennials, I am what is known as a Xennial (a micro-generation born in the late '70s/early '80s) – I love collecting retro analog music such as vinyl records, cassettes, and CDs. I also have approximately 14,000 mp3 files of songs as well (I put all my CDs on my iPod) because I'm aware that times have changed, and I genuinely appreciate how an iPod can benefit music nerds like myself. Again, my favorite shows are retro shows like "Stranger Things" and "The Americans," which are based in the 1980s, but I also love the modern production value of these shows. Watching actual TV shows from the '80s can be fun, but special effects and production value are garbage compared to today, let's be honest. As we get older, there will always be a yearning for the "good 'ole days," but time will never move backward. I think these days, it can be a cool marketing tool and way to differentiate your business to use aspects of the past while maintaining modern digital functionality.

  I say all this about myself because my career is a living example of the *transition* of this revolution. Maybe you are like me and aren't 100% swimming in the digital pool, but also aren't even trying to use these "newfangled gadgets." Let me make one more caveat. We all need to embrace the world around us and understand it, even if we don't fully embrace everything in our personal life. You may not love social media, but you must understand how to use it if you are a business owner. Even better, maybe you can hire a Millennial or someone from Generation Z to run it for you. You may enjoy reading physical copies of books, but if you publish a book or have catalogs of information for your business, you have to also offer it in an e-book or pdf format because a majority of people will be utilizing that format. In most circumstances, offering digital materials to customers and staff is essential to business.

Those who did business like they used to do it in the "good 'ole days" had to quickly change when the Coronavirus Pandemic hit. We had to bring Facetime and video chatting into nursing homes, and many businesses had to upgrade their online presence to stay in business. During any industrial revolution, there will be lines drawn in the sand where a company or individual has to decide to change with the times or fade into obscurity. Even if you find ways to maintain your own identity or relationship to technology, you always want to be aware of the continued changes in the world, and you will be glad you did.

A Word to Millennials and Generation Z

I hope that as you read all these weird perspectives in this chapter that you see it as gaining a historical perspective on the older people around you. They've been through a lot! While Generation X and Xennials have kind of felt caught in the middle of all of this, I know that you probably feel comfortable with the way things currently are. That's great! The business world needs you and your opinions.

It's funny because time just keeps moving, and soon you will be "the old person" talking to my youngest kids

(Generation Alpha) about how it was when you were younger. My oldest (Generation Z) can remember the day they started being able to use an iPad, but my youngest (Generation Alpha) has just always had access to one. One day you will no longer be the young, hip, technological wizard – it will be some other group. Just as you feel like your generation has value and a perspective to offer, so do older generations. With all of the continued technological changes, it's easy to discount those who came before you because their methods seem archaic. As mentioned earlier, technological needs change, but people do not. We all need personalized attention, to feel connected, and desire to have a positive experience when we are spending money. As the world moves forward, we all still need each other and still maintain value regardless of our age.

…and hey Millennials and Generation Z, take it easy on those Generation Alpha kids. It's not their fault that you're so old and out of touch with the "younger generation."

Chapter 10
My Corporate Ladder Is Broken
Large, Small, and Entrepreneur Business

There is an often-unspoken assumption that working for large businesses is the ideal work situation. It used to be that it would allow for more job security, high pay, and the ability to be promoted. My grandfather retired from Goodyear Aerospace after over 35 years, and my great-grandfather retired from Goodyear after about the same amount of time. This longevity and the subsequent ability to live off your retirement were part of the American Dream throughout much of the 1900s.

With the seismic shifts in business approaches due to the rise of the digital age, big business has seen its own changes, and workers have suffered. Growing up in middle America, I have witnessed a few of the largest employers in our area move overseas, regularly downsize, and relocate. Thousands of people in my county lost their formerly secure jobs, sometimes along with their retirement, and then struggled to find a comparable job to replace it with. What do you do when you've had a career for most of your adult life that now does not exist, at least within a viable driving distance? Over the last 30 years, Western society has been changing due to the Third Industrial Revolution and the emergence of the current global economy. Times have changed, and the economic landscape of the world is changing. There are still benefits to working in large corporations, but things are not what they used to be. If you are building your career or assessing your work life, you need to see things for how they are, not just how they have been.

So, is it better to work for a large or a small business? It depends on you and your needs.

"Are you a company man?" That used to be the saying back in the day whenever you would land that stable, potentially lucrative job at the big company near you. It's a question your manager would ask, inquiring if you are willing to do what it takes for the sake of the company succeeding. It implied, "Are you willing to stay late, work long hours, sacrifice your personal life, work for low pay to make more money later, and are you willing to humble yourself to please your boss?" The general idea back then was that your company came first because they provided for you. My grandfather would have been considered a company man: he wore Goodyear hats, bought Goodyear tires, and spoke highly of his company to others. He was proud of where he worked, and I think he loved being a part of something bigger than himself. Along with this "company person" mentality, people like my grandfather were also loyal to brands, grocery stores, department stores, and wherever they worked.

These days, our society has adopted an "every person for themselves" or "I come first" mentality. We are not as loyal to brands and focus on who has the lowest price, highest benefit, or whatever we need. This approach focuses on taking care of yourself or your family first, and the older approach sought to do things that are beneficial to your company (or the business you shop at) that is taking care of you. I believe you should always put yourself and your family first with career and purchasing decisions because no one else is looking out for you. I advocate for shopping at local businesses and supporting your employer with purchases when you can. Still, we should not sacrifice everything valuable to us at the expense of any business. Companies have a bottom line, and at the end of the day, they will make decisions that prioritize profit, not your wellbeing.

There is an incredible diversity of business structures and sizes, so it is nearly impossible to be "specific, general, *and* accurate" when discussing broad categories like this. I will do my best!

In casual conversation, when someone refers to a "small business," they usually mean a scenario where you know your co-workers by name and the leader of the organization is accessible and local, even if they are not available. Some small offices are part of a larger organization, such as a local YMCA office or a medical office that is part of a more extensive medical network. These types of scenarios will fluctuate between my illustrations, but you could say they are usually *culturally* similar to small businesses, but financially they function more like a large business. For the sake of argument, let's define a small business as a place with under 50 employees. When people casually refer to a "large business," they typically mean there are a thousand or more employees, and you may never see the top leader in person. Medium-sized businesses would be anything in between.

Living Large

In comparing the two main entities, there are pluses and minuses to each. When working for large businesses, you will have to deal with rigid corporate policies, limited freedoms, a larger hierarchy, and it will take longer to solve basic problems. In some businesses, everyone works in a cubicle, and only the top executives have their own offices. Unique benefits are that there are more opportunities for promotions and raises, decent retirement and benefits, nice facilities and technical equipment, professional/social respect because you work for a well-known company and clear job duties. One advantage of working for a national organization is that if your office needs to close or make cutbacks, you could be transferred to another city and still keep your position.

Large organizations have many more opportunities for advancement and promotions, which means you can stay there longer. Longevity can be rewarding in some systems. My good friend was doing the exact same job as me, but made about

$30,000 *more* than me because he worked at the company 15 years longer! There is zero exaggeration here. He worked his way up over the years, receiving pay increases, where I came in as the new guy. The disparity in pay was upsetting for my bank account, but what could I say? He put in his time, and it paid off. Ironically, his increases were so gradual, he didn't realize how much his salary had surpassed those around him. Another benefit is that you may have a restaurant, a credit union, or a Starbucks in your office. I used to have a Starbucks about 200 feet from my desk! Since they have big budgets, they may also hold quarterly or yearly events at fancy venues, offering excellent food and drinks. The higher up you are in management, the more opportunities you will have for things like this.

    In terms of salary and perks for top managers, there is no comparison - large businesses are way more lucrative. Most small companies cap out at the $200,000/year range, no matter who you are and what you do. It will bump up a few hundred thousand in a medium-sized business, but still, you can only go so high. This is where small to mid-sized organizations can't compete. CEOs and Vice Presidents in large organizations make several hundred thousand dollars to salaries in the millions per year. A simple internet search will show the average salary for Fortune 500 CEOs with experience under their belt is upwards of $10million. People at the top of their game in this industry are flying first class, if not flying in private jets, living in extraordinary luxury, and have second and third homes in the

Hamptons or Europe.

    A word of caution about those of us who aspire to this level of business leadership: to get to this level, you need top-notch experience, education, unquestioned loyalty, and plenty of quantifiable business success under your leadership. If someone is paying you that much money, the assumption is: this job is your life, and you can perform. Those positions pay that high of salary because you will never stop working and you can deliver what you promise. These are not bad things, per se, but it is not for everyone.

Small but Mighty

    When working for a small business, the average employee will often have to wear multiple hats (doing the job of departments that you do not have, such as accounting, HR, or marketing) and do more than your job description while sometimes receiving a lower salary. It is easier to get your own office, but the need for managing inter-office relationships and small talk is greater. You might have to listen to "Sue" talk every day about her dog or put up with the inter-office drama. The interesting thing is that some smaller to mid-sized businesses have higher pay for entry-level and mid-level jobs than large corporations depending on what type of business it is. In my experience, large businesses are more likely to low-ball your salary offer because they have so many salaries to pay. They have a whole HR department committed to strict guidelines about how much a person can make or how high of a raise you can get. If a small/medium-sized business is doing well for themselves, they may take pride in paying well and try to be competitive with larger businesses. Of course, some small offices may also pay lower than anyone else because their budgets are *also* small. The variance in pay in small to mid-sized businesses is pretty high.

    Regardless, in a small office, business owners are able to make special allowances for their small staff that large businesses can't. While working for large corporations, a random directive to "take the rest of the day off" is almost unheard of, while some generous mid-sized businesses may offer this as something regular during slow times. In small offices around Christmas time, I have often been the recipient of gifts from our customers like gift baskets, tickets to special events, and free meals at area restaurants. I've received $200 cash bonuses at Christmas, just because. If you have a unicorn for a boss, I know of multiple people who use their boss' timeshare or beach house for special events or vacations. These smaller operations often will have excellent benefits (though you may pay more for healthcare itself) and typically more personal/vacation time. Think about it; it is much easier to manage 10 – 50 employees' time-off than managing hundreds or thousands of employees' time-off. I know two small businesses who offer one month of vacation out of the gate – no waiting fifteen to twenty years like there is in a corporate environment! Even after 20 years and holding a high rank in a large organization, you likely won't ever see four weeks of vacation.

Smaller organizations will also tend to offer you your own office and expense account well before a large one would. I had a company credit card, my own office, and a flexible work schedule when I was in my 20s, but my salary wasn't much. I know people who are supervisors of over 100 people in a large business at age 50 with wages in the hundreds of thousands who do not even have their own office. The differences are enormous.

I was working for a small office, which represented a larger progressive organization. I had six people in my office and received a fair salary. One of the benefits of working there was their large contributions to your retirement account. After four years of work, I walked away, having received $25,000 in my retirement account. Looking back, I still can't believe the one month paid time off I got (two weeks sick time, two weeks of vacation time) when my first child was born. That was the same place that sent us home early a couple of times on sunny days and let us work from home on snowy days. They were financially supported by a larger entity, so they could afford extravagant perks. The retirement amount was due to the connection to the larger organization, but the flexibility in time off, the relational atmosphere, and going home for the day were perks of it being a small office.

Top-level positions in small to mid-sized companies often come with decent healthcare and retirement plans, but the flexibility and autonomy are most attractive. Salary ranges can vary greatly but will almost always cap out around $200,000 unless you own the business and things are going really well. Those at the top of their game at this level are more likely to own a big fancy house on a lake with some rental properties or other investments that they get extra income from. When small to mid-sized business owners have next level wealth, typically that has been built from smart investing instead of pure business profit. It is impossible to tell every organization's story and give perfect examples, but hopefully, you can see the differences with the pictures I am painting.

In terms of which type of workplace is best, it all comes down to the industry your business is in, the daily needs of your job, recent profits made, the generosity of those on top, and what you need personally. There is no blanket answer to which is better or what each person prefers. I've had positive and negative experiences in both environments.

"Do It Yourself" Business

While choosing between corporate culture and small business is a complicated decision, those are not your only options! Technological advances like the internet, 3D printers, Square Space, Google business programs (business email, large file sharing, Google search business profiles), and system changes like Amazon.com and Etsy.com have made it easier than ever to start your own small business venture (like selling art on Etsy.com) or becoming an entrepreneur (starting your own business, incorporating it, and running a full operation). The book, *The Passion Economy*,[10] highlights this shift in thinking, showing that it has become a trend for people to pursue their passions instead of just working a job they don't care about. There aren't necessarily more businesses being started, as much as people are finding more and more ways to make a salary from what they love doing.

    I personally started my own non-profit organization and led it for about eight years before changing directions professionally, so I know about starting a small business. My brother-in-law has made a very successful career out of creating his own business model for music education and also working in real estate. The way it looks for each person and business can look very different.

    Starting your own business or service is a lot of work, and there are many risks. The reasons for failure range from lack of experience, bad location, limited marketing, and not knowing how to handle business growth.

    I have a friend who works in the suburbs of a large city, and he designs customized high-end kitchens and bathrooms. He does excellent work and has made hundreds of thousands of dollars doing it. Years ago, he told me that even though he had a steady flow of business and cash, he was not making a profit due to paying other employees and misjudging how long certain jobs would take. How upsetting! He had to mentally step out of himself and his situation, re-evaluate his business plan, and try new approaches. Thankfully, he was able to turn things around and continues to be successful to this day with his new business approach, but he almost lost everything. Having education, specialized mentoring, or a business management background can really make a difference when starting your own business.

Often, a person will start a business because they are good at the specific skill, but they have not had training or experience with running a profitable business. This is why small businesses will hire a business manager or equivalent role, to focus solely on profits to focus on the skill they are best at. You don't need to have a doctorate in business or even a bachelor's degree to succeed, but if you lack formal education, you need to be picking up books, talking to experienced business owners, or hiring someone who can help you thrive. When dealing with your income and your investments, you want to take as few chances as you can.

Assuming you have done your research, have some skills, and know your product, you can find great fulfillment in starting your own business. You may need to put in long hours and be ready to adjust your plans as you go, but if you are doing what you love – it won't feel like "work."

One of the coolest benefits of being your own boss and not having to abide by "company policy" is that you can create your own business culture. If you want to offer extravagant benefits - you can, if you want to give everyone an office or sit in desks in a circle – you can, and if you want to come to work in shorts and a t-shirt – you can. As an entrepreneur, one of the best things is the lack of structure. I have several friends who have worked for a local marketing firm that offers completely casual dress (when not meeting with clients), video games and billiards on breaks, company camping trips, and the freedom to drink beer while working in the office. They wanted to create a fun, casual environment for their business, and they have become quite profitable over the years.

For me, I was able to do most of my work at home or on a big reclining sofa in our building with no shoes on. I dedicated multiple days per week to meet with different people for coffee and had office hours by appointment instead of keeping our facility open 40 hours per week. I worked 50+ hours per week and worked in the afternoons and evenings because that was what worked best for my workstyle - but it wasn't "work" for me; it was enjoyable. I had to find ways to stop working and be present in my personal life. I could work that way because I called the shots on what it looked like, and for us, that served our purposes way better than a traditional model.

In an entrepreneurial setting, you are in charge, so you can call the shots…but when things don't go well, they also fall on your shoulders. You are also responsible for creating a decent work environment for your employees, paying taxes, and providing certain benefits. Lack of structure can be a point of stress for some employees. When hiring people in this environment, it is very important to choose people who understand and already embrace your workstyle and sub-culture. It is also worth noting, especially with growth, that employees tend to crave clear expectations and clear boundaries in their work. The more you can define roles and expectations, the better. While experimenting and pushing traditional workplace boundaries, you also need to ensure a safe working environment and follow governmental guidelines for businesses. In our freedom, we want to make sure that we are also professional, do not unintentionally cross boundaries, and maintain some internal structure. I've found the importance of surrounding yourself with people who aren't like you, yet have a similar vision. It was helpful to me to balance my creative and casual side with people who were practical thinkers because, in the end, it helped things to be both fun and safe.

There are options for which corporate ladder you climb, or whether you climb a ladder at all! You are not doomed to years of servitude just for "a little more time off" or to do work someone else's way for the rest of your life. It's good to know your options before you commit yourself in a certain direction.

Chapter 11
Would You Like Healthcare with That?
Benefits

<u>Well-meaning person</u>: "Well, technically, you're getting paid $7,000 more per year because they are offering you health insurance and other benefits."

<u>Me 15 years ago:</u> "Hmm, interesting. So, with that line of thinking, when I go to pay my rent, I can tell my landlord 'while I don't have actual money to pay you, I can offer you the security of knowing I won't trash your apartment – I'm taking good care of it.' Oh, they won't consider that payment? Me either."

Got Health Insurance?

Ahhh…health insurance. Insurance is the thing that costs a lot of money to have, but if you don't use it, you pretty much paid thousands of dollars for nothing. That would be me. I've paid, I don't know how many thousands of dollars over the course of my life, to have health insurance. I have paid it even though I rarely go to the doctor and have only gone to the hospital one time in the last 20 years - my wife and kids make up for me in that regard. That being said, what is the value of insurance? Why should you care whether or not an employer offers health insurance, a 401k, or other benefits? Per my snarky ignorant comments at the beginning of this chapter, you can see I haven't always appreciated or understood the value of health insurance and benefits. It is also true that these types of benefits...benefit you, the older you get.

The truth of the matter is that health insurance matters, and it *ensures* that you will not have to pay the full out-of-pocket price of healthcare...because healthcare is expensive. We pay doctors, surgeons, medical scientists, and pharmacists well for their services and for the medicine they provide because they allow us to continue to live and not die.

Health insurance seems insignificant until you need it, and when you need it, you really feel the value. It could be the difference of you owing a hospital $20,000 vs. $2,000 or paying $300 for an antibiotic vs. paying $20. It matters in the large scope of your life. Entry-level jobs do not typically come with good benefits. Certain positions offer low pay and limited benefits because those factors are based on experience level, education or training levels, and the skill or responsibility needed to do a particular job. Overseeing other workers, selling high-priced items, ten years of experience, and being required to be on-call 24 hours a day are all variables that go into how much a company pays and how good of benefits you will receive. These factors are not always mirrored in your compensation, but they are significant factors when looking at how organizations decide how much they offer.

While a paycheck is more of an immediate benefit of a job, the other aspects of a benefits package are long term benefits that are not immediately...beneficial. Again, these become more valuable with age and how long you work. Young people don't usually appreciate healthcare and retirement because they typically have fewer medical expenses, and they literally cannot touch retirement for 25 years. This does not mean these benefits are useless – it means you are earning long-term compensation.

For many who are just entering into the workforce or those who find themselves getting older and are now taking notice, it is frustrating that most part-time, retail, and restaurant jobs either come with no insurance or they may offer a costly option for you to purchase separately. The Affordable Care Act (Obamacare) was an attempt to fill this gap of offering health insurance to everyone, despite the level of their employer's goodwill. Unfortunately, while Obamacare helped the average person in many ways (providing "affordable" healthcare for people who could not afford it, free birth control, removing pre-existing conditions), healthcare is still expensive for the average person. This is the heart behind political promises for "healthcare reform" and organizations like Starbucks who offer health insurance to part-time employees. At the time of this writing, healthcare continues to be a problem for scores of U.S. workers.

Benefits

The term "benefits" refers to anything you receive for working that is not cash. At first glance, these things may not be exciting, but it's one of the great things about higher-level jobs, especially if you persevere and stay awhile at your company. Let me be clear: a job with excellent benefits can sometimes be the difference between a job being "okay" vs. being "an amazing job."

Besides your salary, things to keep in mind when looking at what a position offers: **1. Health insurance**: Something to note about your health insurance plan is how much you will pay each month out of your check for coverage. People pay anywhere from zero to $50 per pay, to $400 or more, depending on your coverage. Again, health insurance won't pay your bills, but it could save you from paying tens of thousands of dollars to a hospital. **2. Holidays, Vacation, Personal, and Sick Days:** These are days where you don't work – because it's a holiday, you are on vacation, or you are sick - but you will still get paid. The number of days you are offered to be paid for not working is just free money, so those are valuable. **3. Special Benefits**: Depending on your industry, some businesses offer really great perks. Working for a college can usually get someone in your household free college classes. Working for a car manufacturer can usually get discounts on cars, and some food service businesses will offer free or discounted food. Some large companies I have worked for offered a discount on my cell phone bill through Verizon. **4. 401k** (or other investment options) and **profit-sharing** are very valuable if you plan on staying at this place for longer than a couple of years. When an employer contributes to your 401k, that means they are paying into a savings account for you. Sometimes the accounts that are set up are not accessible until you are over 55 years old, but for those of us who are not great at saving, it forces you to save for the future. Profit-sharing means that when the company makes extra profits, then you will too. Sometimes this works to your benefit a little (meaning you make a couple hundred dollars extra per year), or on a rare occasion, it works *greatly* to your advantage (a person may retire from a company after 20 years as a millionaire because the company made a lot of money and they never touched it over the years). This scenario greatly depends on who you work for, how much of a percentage you receive, and whether or not you actually save this money and let it keep accumulating.

      Let's take a moment and apply some simple math for those of us who are new to this concept. $5,000 in your hand today is $5,000 in your hand tomorrow. Now, if you invest $5,000 at 5% earning each year, in 20 years, you will have $10,000. There are many variables involved, but in this environment, it literally pays to save for the future.

      All in all, benefits are rooted in your future. If you want long term success and health, it is crucial to think about your future instead of what you can get right now.

Chapter 12
Me, Myself, and Hi
Job Interviews and Resumes

It's about the story you tell. At first glance, a cover letter/resume and job interview are, in essence, answering a series of questions and just being honest about your job history. Unfortunately, this won't get you hired in of itself; in fact, it could quickly get you tossed aside.

First, a resume documents the facts of your employment history. It should contain low embellishment, but it is helpful to quantify (assigning a number to) things like how many years you have done management, sales, customer service, or how much you have sold. A cover letter is a *one-page* summary of your work history, your goals, and why you are the best person for this job. A job interview is where you show them you are the person described in your application and demonstrate your competencies. If you get an interview, that means your cover letter and resume were effective. If you get a second interview, that means your first interview was effective.

You need to see your interviews and cover letter/resume as a story you are telling. For a sales position, you tell the story of your life and how you could sell yellow snow to an Eskimo (you can sell anything to anyone). Their number one concern is "can this person sell something?" and you want them to take one look at your resume/cover letter and say, "oh, here we go – they sold X amount of this, and X amount of that in X amount of time." That is how you get an interview, and then you continue with that storyline. For both your cover letter and interview content, you want to pull this data from your resume. You don't want to lie or exaggerate – you want to find the parts of your life story to highlight. Truly, it sometimes takes time to see your own value and "life metrics."

For a management position, you will be telling the story of how, everywhere you go, you manage things and people. You want to pull out the times you managed budgets, led a team, kept calm in a stressful situation, and of course, any management titles you have had (team manager, lead designer).

You aren't *making up a story* about yourself, but instead telling *your story*, using your unique experiences and highlighting your accomplishments. I say all this because often we don't see our own potential and are overly focused on the details of our job history (my boss was demanding, I didn't hit this goal, I didn't get paid what I was worth) instead of what we have accomplished and our quantified experience. Some of us are too honest - beyond what they are looking for. For anyone who needs to hear this: interviews are not "tell-all" situations where you recount what you have done wrong or what you didn't like. They want to know the honest truth about what you have done right and what you do well, along with a small sample of your weak spots. Obviously, if you aren't good at something, you shouldn't apply for a job doing that thing!

When trying to apply for a job outside of your experience, but you want to head in that direction, you may need to spend some extra time analyzing your experiences from an outside perspective. One time, I was asked if I had any sales experience, and my first thought was "no." I failed to remember the $60,000+ I had raised by myself over the course of a year to start my own organization! My memory always focused on what I did *after* I raised the money, but even though my title wasn't "sales manager," I was selling an idea and was quite successful! I also forgot that I had retail management experience, which included sales, but again "sales" wasn't in my title. So, it turned out that I had some basic sales background and some unique sales experience! Take some time, and make sure you are highlighting those experiences.

If you can get an interview, you want to put those experiences and highlights in your heart and continue to tell your story with some confidence, knowing you are the kind of person they are looking for.

Another important point when applying for a position is noting what the job advertisement lists as key responsibilities and what experience they want you to have had. When writing your resume and cover letter, you want to respond to those points either directly or indirectly. If you get an interview, you want to keep those points in mind when answering questions - they are looking for a certain type of person with a particular background.

Interview Questions

This may be obvious, but let me say that no interview is merely about answering the questions "right" unless you are taking some type of competency exam. Every interview is a test to see if you are the right *fit* for their organization and this position. You could answer every question the way they want, be charming, and look professional, but you will not get the job if you are 10 minutes late. If you are qualified but argue with the interviewer, you are not likely to get the position. You could *not* answer everything perfectly, but if you are the type of person they are looking for and get along with you, you may either get a second interview or get the job anyway. In an interview, the main questions they are trying to answer in their minds about you is whether they will get along with you and if you will still be working there in a year. Hiring, training, and paying you - only to have you leave in four months is not what they want (unless it's a short-term job). You are an investment, and they want to know if you are worth investing in.

It is worth noting that interviews and questions will vary depending on what type of work and what type of position you are going for. You need to enter into the situation knowing this information. Much of this information can be gleaned from their website, message boards, or websites like Indeed and Glassdoor that will either say they are 'casual,' or you may be able to read about other people who have interviewed there.

Many places will start with, "Tell me about yourself." This is an invitation to either highlight those unique things about you that hopefully align with the company's priorities or to give a brief background of how you got there professionally. They may want to hear how you got interested in the field you are applying for, and this would be a good time to quickly beat them to the punchline of things like "While I don't have a long background in sales, I have realized that is what I want to do with my career…" No matter what, keep your introduction to less than 3 minutes or so. Brief. To the point.

Keep in mind that, unless you know the interviewer personally, they do not know you at all. In their mind, you could be a crazy person, and they are trying to figure that out. They typically won't take everything you say at face value. Some questions are intended to throw you off your prepared answers so that you will show your true colors.

Throwing you off

More and more, interviewers are using the interviewing tactic of throwing you off your prepared answers. They do this to see who you really are. This is what is known as a disruptive question or a disruptive approach. I'm not a big fan of this approach because a person could be a good fit for a position but just not respond to being thrown off like you want them to. I know some great workers who, upon sensing humiliation coming, just shut down. I also know some great workers who are unphased by any interview scenario. The problem is that narrow-minded interviewers sometimes pass by someone genuinely great simply because they are a unique person with a unique background.

Back in the day, the dreaded disruptive question used to commonly sound like "If you were a fruit/candy/vegetable, what would you be?" The intended use of that question was to see if a person could think on their feet or see if they could be fun, and you could find out subconscious information. I guess they were hoping to hear, "I would be a strawberry because I'm so sweet!" *twists pointer finger into cheek with a cute smile* or maybe "I would be coffee candy because I'm bitter under the surface" *womp, womp, whaahhh*. Sorry, but identifying yourself with a specific food has nothing to do with a person's fun or creative side (I would say that makes you the opposite!). As an interviewer, you should be able to read people better or ask better questions if you want more information. Perhaps a better disruptive question would be, "Tell me something you do for fun." There you go - done.

True story: I was part of an interviewing team, and someone asked what they do for fun, and they said very sternly, "I don't do anything for fun. My kids take up all of my extra time. I'm too busy with all the things I have going on to relax. I wish I had more time, but I just don't." We all just sat there, not knowing what to say. Note: never say that because it makes you look crazy. There is an example of a disruptive question doing its job!

Mall Madness: I once heard from one of my students that they interviewed in the mall for a shoe store job, and the interviewer sent them and someone else who was interviewing on a scavenger hunt around the mall. The winner got the job. Yikes!

Keep It Positive and Specific

When it comes to previous work experience: Keep it positive. Talking negatively about others in an interview is always a red flag that *you* are trouble. If you are willing to talk crap about your previous co-workers, they can anticipate you will do the same to them in the future. The younger you are, the more likely they will take the side of your previous employer. It's nothing personal; it's just that many young people will blame their supervisors for their own ignorance or poor job performance.

If they ask why you are leaving your previous job, don't tell them that it's because your current boss is a jerk. You should point towards your career goals and what they have to offer. If they ask what it is about your current job you don't like, again, try to keep it positive and focus on something general. Often interviewers will use what you say to decide if you are the right fit. For instance, if you say, "It's too crazy and busy," they might conclude that you can't handle busyness. I say this because I had an interviewer tell me that! If you say, "My supervisor is always harping on me about my performance, but I'm doing a good job!" many interviewers will read that example as "This person has job performance issues." Keep it positive, so they don't misread you.

The most common types of questions for any job will be questions about the specific experiences you have had. "Tell me about a time that you exceeded your sales goals," "Tell me about a time you went above and beyond to give great customer service," or "How would you handle the following scenario…". What they are looking for are not quick answers, but *quantifiable* answers and preferably a short work anecdote or story that shows how you handled that scenario. Here is an example of what they are looking for, "One time I had a customer who didn't receive what they ordered (name specific item), so I apologized for their negative experience and told them I would take care of them. I spoke with my manager, resolved it (giving quick examples of what you did), and gave the customer a coupon for a free (specific) service for the next time they order from us. The customer was very satisfied when they walked away." That is specific, explains what you did and how you did it, and how it was resolved. You want to show them a 360 view of your skills, including your interactions with your manager and the customer (or whatever the scenario is).

Next-Level Job Interview Checklist:

1. *Be Early*: Arrive early no matter what. Take a moment to take deep breaths, so you are ready to have a calm, confident conversation.
2. *Dress the part*: Always dress at least slightly above what you would wear daily to the job.
3. *Act the part*: You need to act and respond like someone who knows the job and is comfortable in their own skin.
4. *Questions*: Have some answers prepared based on what you anticipate being asked, noting your specific experiences. Have at least three questions to ask them at the end about their company or the job itself. Good questions are, "What would a typical day look like in this job?" or specific questions that show you know what to expect, like "How many accounts would I be responsible for?"
5. *Confidence*: Practice in the mirror or practice with a friend or significant other. Think and speak in full sentences, meaning you should speak clearly and end whatever thoughts you start.
6. *Please Do*: Research the company online, know your interviewer's name and use it, and accept their offers of things like water, coffee, or special drink even if you don't drink it. Some places will use this as a way to see if you are friendly and open.

7. *Entry-level positions*: You want to convince them that you can follow directions and think for yourself. Think of an example to share.
8. *Management positions*: You want to convince them that you can give direction and motivate a group of people. Think of examples to share.
9. *Top-level managers*: You want to be sure you know all about the company, and even details about their vision, quarterly reports, etc.

Chapter 13
I'm Going to Be a YouTuber
What's a Back-up Career?

When I was in high school, I was singularly focused, and my parents told me, "James, you need a back-up career in case your perfect scenario doesn't work out." This was so offensive to me! How could they say that and not believe in me? Well, it turns out that they were right, but not in the way any of us anticipated. I'll explain.

I had a goal to start an organization to help people, and I was laser-focused on it. Along the way, I continued to need rent money and food, go figure. I got married, worked, and kept pursuing my goals. Even though I didn't grow up with a computer, in Chicago, I continued to find administrative jobs where I was working a lot with computers and technology. I found myself building webpages, managing websites, getting organizations on social media, and digitizing their businesses. A skill that I didn't even know that I had 20 years ago ended up being one of the most essential skill sets in my professional toolbox. I used these skills in the career I was pursuing and also in the jobs I did to pay my bills.

After working for community organizations and

churches for seven years, I started my own community based non-profit organization. That was my vision, my career goal, and my WorkTopia. It was a success, and I can say that I did it. It was difficult, though, and it took a toll on my personal life. After eight years of leading this non-profit, my life changed, and I found myself needing to head in a different direction. I was heartbroken, but I had to do what I had to do.

I didn't have a back-up plan, but I did have skills and other types of work on my resume that I could use. Since then, I have been able to find ways to use my gifts and talents to build a career and a life for my family. I didn't know things would change so much within fifteen years, but they did.

No one knows the future, and I would never suggest that someone "plan to fail," but I have seen enough of life to know that rarely does life go the way we expect. It doesn't always have to go *bad*, but as I discuss elsewhere in this book, the business world has been changing at break-neck speed for quite some time now. Whether you take a couple of college classes that are different from what you are aiming for, or you do some part-time work doing something different from you usually have done, all knowledge and experience can be useful in the end.

As someone who has given his whole young adult life to following his dreams and then achieved them, I can tell you that if you are passionate about something and have what it takes to get it done – go for it and don't let anyone tell you that you can't.

As you pursue these things, you may need to work a second job or do some side work to pay the bills. While you can't worry about failure and also focus on success, it is important to come to terms with reality: all great ideas aren't lifelong payouts. You may create a product or launch a cool store, but it may not fully support you 30 years from then. Think of famous actors who continued to go to college or famous restaurants that ended up closing – **having a back-up plan isn't planning to fail; it's ensuring long term success**. Professional success doesn't mean you will be doing the same thing for the rest of your life; in fact, professional success usually means you *don't* do the same thing for the rest of your life. We must continue evolving upward as professionals in order to thrive.

Chapter 14
It's Not You, It's Me…It's Mostly You, Though
Rejection

"Fall down seven times, stand up eight" – Japanese proverb

Don't feel bad. The odds are, no matter how hard you fail or are rejected, someone has likely failed or been rejected harder. I've felt the sting of regret ("I shouldn't have said that") and rejections that made me feel like I'm not good enough.

Whether you are not getting calls for interviews after you submit your resume, have not gotten multiple jobs after interviews, are getting corrective action at work, or even have gotten let go…rejection is painful. It is even painful when you *know* it's not your fault. One time an interviewer, upon looking at my resume, bristled and almost with a tone of me being a fraud, asked what a Bachelor of Arts degree was. "I know what a Bachelor of Science is, but is Bachelor of Arts a college degree?" Yes, the person interviewing me and subsequently, the interviewer who *didn't* hire me, knew so little that she thought I was trying to pull a fast one on her. I got rejected, quite possibly because she didn't know how college degrees worked. I still get frustrated when I think about that conversation.

What is it about rejection that feels so bad? Catch this: a

psychologist friend of mine said that the feeling of rejection feels so bad because the same areas of the brain become activated when we are rejected as when we experience physical pain. MRI studies on brain activity show that rejection hurts so bad (neurologically speaking) because it registers the same as physical pain in your brain. Strangely enough, if you take pain reliever before being rejected, you will handle the rejection better. Wow! The good news is that rejection can build resilience if we don't allow it to destroy us, and we keep moving forward. If you can let go, refocus, move on, forgive, or whatever you need to do – you can let your rejections build character and personal strength.

    I would encourage you, especially if you have several rejections or have gotten fired, to seek wisdom from trusted friends or someone older. It might be a good idea to have them look over your resume, give you some pointers, or even run some of your interview answers by them. Especially when getting fired or laid off, it would be a good idea to seek counsel from someone older. Often, we are angry at the injustice or misunderstandings and miss what we could have done differently. Either way, we have all made mistakes, and you have the opportunity to get back up and try again.

Feeling alone? Let these highly publicized rejections keep you company:

- J.K. Rowling's Harry Potter book was rejected by 12 different publishers. Bloomsbury Publishing went as far as to tell her, "Don't quit your day job." Hopefully, J.K. has found a way to comfort herself by the 500 million copies sold in her Harry Potter series.
- After just one performance, Elvis Presley ("the King of Rock n' Roll") was fired by the Grand Ole Opry with the endearing message of, "You ain't going nowhere, son. You ought to go back driving a truck."
- Stephen King's first novel, "Carrie," was rejected…wait for it…THIRTY times before it was published. That book alone has sold about 350 million copies.
- Thomas Edison, you know the guy who gave us electricity in our homes, was fired from Western Union after he spilled Sulfuric acid on the floor. With his extra time he then had, he invented the lightbulb…which could have helped everyone avoid the hole he created in the Western Union floor.
- Vincent Van Gogh, considered one of the greatest painters of all time, only sold one of his paintings in his lifetime.
- Oprah Winfrey was fired from her job as a TV reporter because she was "unfit for TV." A billion dollars later, now she has her own network.

Rejection hurts, it really does, but we need to find ways to let our rejections fuel our passion to try harder and hone our skills.

While you may not become an overnight success or a millionaire, you could become successful being you and doing what you love. We can't let rejection define us because you are unique, and not everyone will see our value at first glance.

Chapter 15
Working from Home: "Thank You, Coronavirus!"

Within the world of office work, working from home used to be a coveted and unique privilege. People used to use that as an in-your-face exclamation at the end of their resignation ("I'm quitting. I got a job where I can work-from-home!"). Enter COVID-19, and suddenly a couple of months later, a majority of employed adults said they worked from home on some level. The 2020 Pandemic changed the way we all work – and suddenly, some companies realized it was a viable long-term option, cutting down on overhead, utilities, and physical resources.

    Depending on your type of work and personality, working from home can either be enjoyable, miserable, or somewhere in between. What held many organizations back from allowing employees to work from home ranged from necessary face-to-face contact, technological limitations, and a general sense of mistrust that employees are doing what they are supposed to be doing. The governmental quarantine mandates quickly forced organizations to adopt this new approach or close down.

Work for Success at Home

In lieu of trust, some managers enforce that you maintain an "online" status for those working on laptops or some other form of proof, which can be a challenge for various reasons. One solution people have found are little apps you can download, such as "Mouse Jiggler," that keep your laptop from going to screen saver if you aren't actively moving the mouse. This could encourage abuse, but it could also be a benefit to people who are available, but on the phone, or need to step away for a few moments like you would in the office.

Another emotionally variable topic is the issue of what to wear while working from home. If you are on Zoom/Skype video calls, you need to be presentable from the waist up, but what about when you aren't doing video calls? The general law of the universe that says, "dress for success" and "getting dressed up makes people feel good" seem to have bearing here. Many people encourage those who work from home to continue to shower in the morning and get ready as if you were going to see people, even if you are by yourself at home. This encourages a healthier mindset, and things like taking walks and stepping away from your computer are essential work-from-home routines to keep. These principles are more about mental and emotional health that ultimately will help you in your job performance.

Whether you have a mansion, a 1-bedroom apartment, or your perfect home office, it is vital to invest in your success. Aside from getting up early, showering, getting dressed, drinking coffee, and greeting others…you want to make sure you have the right tools. You can find comfy office chairs online for less than $100, a small desk for less than $150, and a nice big computer screen for less than $150. You don't have to break the bank to get some useful tools for work success. Some businesses will even order some of these things for you. If you can be intentional upfront, it will pay off in the long run.

Projecting Positivity

One of the downsides to working from home is that even though you might be buried in work, if you seem unwilling to do "more" you might be met with silent suspicion that you are being lazy. I have found that **you always want to appear available, and you always need to be willing**. What that means is, even if you are buried in work and on the phone constantly, it is not a good idea to just tell your boss, "No, I'm too busy." It's better to say something like, "Okay, sure, I'm willing to do what needs to be done, but can we talk about my workload soon? My workload feels high." You should then quantify your workload, so they understand (I have *this many* accounts; I'm working after hours already, etc.). Unfortunately, when you are not visible, you are at the mercy of your supervisor's imagination.

Conversely, sometimes you are caught off guard, and

your boss reaches out to you, and you are knee-deep in some non-work-related activity. You need to be on it and drop whatever it is that you are doing. You could be taking a shower and eating cheese puffs, but if your supervisor says they need something from you – you say, "I'm on it. I'll have it to you as soon as possible!" Then you drop the Cheetos, grab a towel, and get it done! Working from home will inevitably enable you to become distracted or to be in uniquely compromising situations. Still, it is important to be "on" whenever you are needed – which is what they are paying you for, of course.

Many jobs will do morning check-ins over Zoom or phone, where your team gets a morning pep talk or your marching orders. This may be annoying to you, but again, you aren't being asked to go into the office, so you should see this as payment for that, or at best, you can see it as a morning pep talk. This goes without saying, but this would not be the time to talk about still being in bed. You also want to make sure your phone is on mute if you are running kids around. Don't be like me, who accidentally bumped my mute button and had a whole interaction with my youngest about giving me a kiss and her screaming in her car seat about wanting her blanket. I'm sure it sounded completely insane, but I didn't realize I was sharing my crazy moment with 20 other people until my boss was like, "James…go on mute!"

Some of us have home offices, some of us have kids who are always around, and some of us are easily distracted –

unfortunately, none of those factors matter in the end. If you work from home, you will be competing with people from potentially better working scenarios than you. Some people thrive in this environment, and some people do not – it comes down to personality type, workstyles, and life situations. Do your best to maintain an air of peace and calm when you can.

Work-from-home Guilt

Working from home is a blessing and a curse. The blessing is that you can multi-task, wear what you want, and take breaks when you need them. The curse of it is that you sometimes feel like your work is never done. You can always pick up the computer and do that last task or make up for not doing enough earlier. There is something I'll call "Work-from-Home Guilt," which is the feeling you get when you've spent too much time slacking, and so, you pick up your laptop and work into the night. It may all balance out in the end, but studies show that it might not. People tend to work more when they work from home in general. This can turn into a cycle that eats up your whole day, and you never truly get a break.

Make sure that you set up boundaries if you work from home. As I said, start your day right and get a shower, drink some coffee, start on time, do your work, take breaks, and then have a stopping time. If you work in the evening because you need to, make sure you set an end time to spend some time being a human and are then ready to go the next day. If you are always working late, it will continue into a vicious cycle where you are never truly "off work." Being off work allows you to recharge.

Let working-from-home be the blessing that it can be. If you keep yourself accountable in the important moments, you can enjoy it safely when the natural "downtime" occurs.

Chapter 16
Teamwork Makes the Dream Work

When I was in school, I would hear my fellow students say things like, "Group work is so dumb – in the real world, you don't have to do things like this." It's funny, though, because nothing could be farther from the truth! You will likely work in teams for your entire life, with few exceptions. That's why you don't listen to "Tyler" because Tyler doesn't know what the heck he is talking about. Here are a few jobs that depend on teamwork: anything in the medical field, the construction field, sales, management, sports, office management, non-profit work, project management, manufacturing, logistics, and foodservice. So, like, everything.

    I remember one of my first experiences with different departments. I was an assistant to the head accounting director, and he would have me ask for things from accounting. 100% of the time, their response began with a sigh. Their frustration would come at me, and I felt like such an annoying person even though I literally had no idea what I was even asking for. When I would tell the manager I was working for about that, he would say, "Well that's their job – they are lazy over there and don't seem to understand what their actual job is." I didn't know what to think because they didn't seem lazy, but over time I began to see similar exchanges, and it convinced me that there was something wrong with "them." The "us versus them" attitude is everywhere.

When I started assisting those same people in accounting, I began seeing why they hated those requests so bad. They would have stacks of papers about 12 inches tall, and they would be processing that stack…page by page…typing it into a computer…number after number, page after page, number after number…STOP…look up at this 19-year-old asking them to dig through the stack they processed three days ago that has been filed away down the hall…knowing that they would have to find their place again among that stack and those numbers…to get through the rest of the pile on their desk so they could go home. My interruptions would slow them down and often make it, so they had to stay later. *Ohhhhhh.* After that, I saw the supervisor's simple requests differently. It was still their job, but sometimes simple questions can affect a person's whole day.

There are different types of teams, but the broadest category would be 'formal' and 'informal teams.' Formal teams are when you are assigned to work together, whereas informal teams are when you self-group based on things like proximity or you have co-workers who you depend on. Generally speaking, most of your positions will be benefitted from being a "team player," as they say. In an interview or resume, that is always a positive phrase to throw around because it shows that you recognize the reality of needing to work well with others.

Exploring Foreign Lands (Departments)

Most offices, businesses, and professions group employees by functionality. There might be one person who performs those functions, or maybe there is a room full of people doing it. Much like trying to find a place to eat in the cafeteria on a cliché high school TV show, when walking into these departments, you are faced with a group of similar people – the nerds, the jocks, the popular kids, the cool kids, and the subcategories go on. Some of the most common departments are Human Resources (HR), Accounting / Accounts Payable, Sales, Management, Customer Service, Information Technology (IT), and Manufacturing. There are so many possibilities depending on what your industry is, but you get the idea. Typically, people in each category are naturally certain personality types or temperaments – not 100% of the time, but like 95% of the time.

In any job, especially if there is tension between departments, you will want to gradually build relationships with everyone - so that when you need it, they will *want* to help you. Each department needs a different approach. I've worked in most of these departments, so I've seen some things. Please indulge me while I over-simplify human emotions and behavior into potentially offensive little boxes:

When you need something from **accounting or accounts payable**, you want to be kind and measured because they deal with numbers all day. They could probably use some pleasant human interaction even if they aren't super-expressive. They are usually in the middle of something, so yes, you are always interrupting. It usually takes a second for them to register what you want because they are up to their eyeballs in tasks and processes.

People in **I.T. (Information Technology)** are just like anyone else in that they both enjoy being productive but also love what they love. What makes a person a "nerd" is having passion for ultra-specific things. They might seem quiet because the general idea is that they feel like no one understands or cares about their ultra-specific things. Suppose you want to build a positive relationship with someone in this department, and you are waiting around. In that case, you could always ask if they saw the latest Star Wars (or equivalent pop culture phenomena) movie or show – or if you are familiar with video games, ask their thoughts about that. Your expectation should be that they will make a dissenting remark about it because "This is the way" (Star Wars joke). If they have little toys or comic book figures on their desk, they usually can't resist if you bring up nerd topics like Star Wars, comic books, video games, and how Hollywood has watered down their favorite childhood interests. Unlike people in other departments, they often talk about highly specialized topics with passion while doing highly technical tasks on a computer because they have grown up doing this exact thing.

When dealing with **upper-level management**, you can gain some favor by being willing to address problems yourself, getting to the point, and not wasting their time. They have high-pressure jobs to do, so it's helpful to them if you sometimes write your question down before you walk into their office, so you *get to the point*. They don't usually need the backstory, just the question. The quickest way to annoy someone in management is to tell them "the whole story" or include them in the nuances of the drama. I promise they don't want to hear about the drama, but they want to solve your problem.

If you are speaking with **HR (Human Resources)**, you will want to keep your inappropriate jokes and sarcasm to a minimum, as it is their job to ensure interpersonal appropriateness and sign your paychecks. They are used to people being cautious around them, so you also don't want to stand out as crass or clueless. It is worth noting that they often deal with serious employee issues within the office and have to have difficult conversations with people, so give them some grace if they seem a little uptight.

Different Function – Same Team

Let's say you are in some type of sales or project management role, and a month after the product is delivered, the customer calls and says they already paid their bill and want to know why they are getting another one. You will likely be asking someone in Accounts Payable / Billing / Accounting about if it has been paid or what the scenario was the customer referring to. What if a customer orders something, and while you were told it would be completed in manufacturing two weeks ago, you are still waiting for it to be completed?

Take either of those scenarios and then put yourself in the other person's shoes. If someone comes at you kindly, with grace and understanding, and asks for the status on a billing or manufacturing issue – you will feel the freedom to do your job and get them what they need. On the other hand, if they come at you with verbal frustration and even make small jabs at you, acting like you didn't do your job, you will feel a little attacked, and suddenly there is a conflict with someone from another department. When you two are done with that interaction, do you know what will happen after that? You will both go back to what you were doing…destined to have a similar conversation next week, next month, or in 2 hours.

If you are on the same team and it is a regular part of your job, it's not wise to treat people in the other departments with attitude or to look down on them (especially if, as is customary, everyone in your department talks bad about that department). That is toxic behavior.

Think about the difference between ending your request with "I need this now" versus "I know this is annoying, but this customer seems upset. How long do you think it will take?" One person seems to be demanding and a little offensive, and one person sounds like a team member. When dealing with job stress and other co-workers, try to keep your stress out of your interactions – and point the *focus* of your stress *away* from your co-worker interactions instead of allowing them to wonder if you are mad at *them*. When the next problem arises, guess who you have to interact with again? If you interact with them kindly and with some personal touches, you will start building relationships with them – which ultimately may lead to them going the extra mile for you when it counts.

    I'll be honest; I have not always been the best at every one of my jobs. I've spent years *trying my best* only to find out my best isn't as good as I would have liked. Do you know what has saved me, though? Relationships with co-workers. If you keep a perspective that "We're in this together, I've got your back" and making sure you help them when they ask you as well, something strange and mysterious happens: your "work" becomes "teamwork," and yes, Tyler, your "teamwork" …ultimately, makes the "dream work." *He says with a wink and a "ding"* *

    The pseudo-inspirational joke-phrase, "teamwork makes the dream work," is a little silly, but it's true. When you work together as a team, you can accomplish greater things than you could accomplish by yourself. If the numbers person is working with numbers, the relationship person manages relationships, and the builders are manufacturing the product, then the end result is productivity, full functionality, and success! Even when people around you constantly reference how another department is [fill in the blank, negative thing], you can still treat others with respect and even defend them a little. Sure, some people don't do their jobs, or their actions affect our jobs, and that is frustrating – but the more you dig into your differences, the less productive you will be.

    Now, with that being said, how do comments like "I just want to do the work by myself; you don't have group work in the real world" sound? That attitude is out of touch and concerning if you need to depend on that person for your own performance. Working in teams can be difficult, but if done well, it can be a really rewarding and fun process. Take that "Tyler."

Section III: Rising to the Top

Chapter 17
You Can Dooo It!

This third section is intended to teach you how to think and act like a leader and explain some essential dynamics of leadership. Some of us have dreams of becoming a great leader, and others of us simply don't see ourselves that way.

Nine years before I was speaking to hundreds of people about my vision for the organization I wanted to start, and twenty years before I started teaching classes about leadership dynamics, I could barely envision leading other people. I didn't come from a family with management jobs, so I had a hard time envisioning what it would even look like for myself.

I wrestled with how I could consider being in a leadership role when I did not feel 'better' than anyone else? I couldn't get over the idea of having authority over others as I was the youngest in my family and didn't think very highly of myself.

Being a manager or a leader is not about being outgoing, better than anyone else, or being a narcissist. It is about having a different job function. In every organization, there are people who clean and maintain the building, people who keep track of administrative details, people who have more customer service or core function jobs, and then people who manage and lead the organization. Everyone's role is important in helping an organization run well. Some positions have big picture responsibilities, and some have more day-to-day maintenance responsibilities. There are even different types of leaders who have varied duties. Some leaders lead small teams doing one function, while others lead the whole organization.

Leaders do and should think differently. They should have different priorities and have unique responsibilities. Unfortunately, many poor leaders are in their positions due to "ending up" in them instead of it being because they understand the world around them. Be intentional! Knowledge and perspective can make you a better leader and will ultimately make it easier for you to rise to the top!

Chapter 18
Every Person the Light Touches
Vital Elements of Management

Have you ever wondered why supervisors get paid so much more than everyone else? Is it an unfair position to be in? Being a supervisor in management calls for higher pay because of the impact they are supposed to have. The goal of management is for one person to impact a group of people and to increase their productivity and success.

It has been widely taught that a manager's job revolves around four main topics:

Planning – Organizing – Leading – Controlling

1. **Planning:** The first step is to decide things like what you are doing, what you need to get it done, and estimating time frames. When you run a long race, you think through the course – planning how much energy you need or your speed you use to deal with hills, woods, straightaways, and making it to the finish line. If you do not plan ahead in business, you are at the mercy of supply chains, your competition, the economy, and your employees. Any one of those areas can

knock your vision off the tracks. The more prepared you are with a business plan, the more likely you are to succeed.

2. **Organizing:** This step is getting everything in order, identifying positions and appointing people to lead, and deciding where each piece goes. If you were going to build a car from scratch, you could go to a car parts store or a junkyard and find the hundreds of pieces, throwing them in a big pile. That approach would be a disaster! You would want to sort the pieces based on what part of the car you are building, most likely putting nuts and bolts in one pile while the large pieces go in another. The same is true with taking a test – you want to have everything you need in the right place to optimize your precious time. Organizing is a way to prepare resources and anticipate the twists and turns of your business plan. Henry Ford (of Ford Motors) and McDonalds focused on organizing their businesses and perfected the assembly line concept used by the world today. Organization allowed them to save enormous amounts of time and money, which benefitted everyone.

3. **Leading:** Once you have a plan, and you know who needs to do what, and your supplies are in place, you start the process. Leaders should regularly be pointing towards the goal and the vision. Great leaders find ways to motivate so that others naturally want to follow them. If you had ten dogs and you needed to get out of the house and into a car, the distraction possibilities are endless for each dog. If you

open the front door, show them several steaks you made, and toss them in your car – your task will be complete in seconds. People are much harder to motivate than dogs, but everyone is motivated by certain things. Leaders find appropriate motivations for others and then point towards the goal, reminding and encouraging them along the way.

4. **Controlling:** The last step is maintaining or making adjustments as needed. You may increase work in certain areas and pull back in others, refocus your attention, or take something back to the drawing board. When landline phones began losing their appeal, businesses like AT&T had to re-evaluate their entire revenue stream. They still offer landline access, but that is no longer their focus. It could have been the end of their business entirely if they hadn't decided to put more energy into internet and cell phone development. When problem areas are identified, they need taken back through the process of Planning, Organizing, Leading, and then Controlling. Controlling is where many of us spend the bulk of our time, trying to keep everything moving, making small adjustments, and looking ahead to anticipate changes.

In large businesses, it is very rare for you to be involved in the organization's Planning and Organizing process. Still, you may be interested in this process regarding a new department or new objective/product launch. We all see the Controlling aspect as you are asked to tighten your budget, evaluate a process, or when a supervisor does regular performance reviews. The smaller the organization, the more likely you will be involved in each aspect of this process.

If you are in the controlling stage, you need to go back to the planning stage, that you have not failed – that is what keeps organizations alive and thriving! It should be a living process. Organizations that stop adjusting, evaluating, and restructuring are doomed to die eventually. All living things change or adapt to survive, and an organization is no different. Our culture, the product market, consumers, and our larger economy are constantly in flux. Sometimes it is very subtle, like a gradual decrease in customer traffic at the mall, and other times there may be a seismic shift such as with the invention of the internet or the Coronavirus Pandemic.

Whether the issue is that people just don't like Crocs anymore, they prefer shopping online, or cities are locked down due to a health crisis, businesses must respond and even anticipate change in order to thrive. During these more obvious shifts, you will see companies going bankrupt or downsizing, while others find a new path through innovation to either maintain or grow. In my lifetime, I have seen this happen in a number of industries. There was a time in the 1990s when it was super cool to go to 'sit down' coffee shops and bookstores with cozy chairs, and movie rental stores were the place to go for "on demand" movies. These businesses came to a screeching halt in the 2010s due to the subsequent popularity of drive-through coffee shops, online shopping, and even movies in the theater being offered on streaming services. This is not a new phenomenon! There have always been business trends where new models explode with growth, while others just explode – more specifically, lose money and have to close. Managers are the ones who had to make those decisions - to either control and maintain or go back to planning/re-evaluating and make changes.

Management

There are different types of managers, and their functions are not all the same. When you take on a management role or when you are working closely with someone in a management role, it is helpful to recognize what level you/they are in:

Levels of Management

Top Managers (CEO, President, VP) focus on the organization's big picture, maintaining the vision and direction. They manage public image, investors, the future of the company, and maintaining profitability.

Middle Managers (Department Managers, Store Managers, Foremen, Assistant Managers) carry out the Top Managers' vision, plan and organize departmental needs, and oversee first-line managers. They report to Top Managers about finances and how employees are performing in broad strokes. These managers often keep track of time-off, assign positions, do performance reviews, and take responsibility if someone doesn't show up for a shift. Middle managers are notorious for feeling "caught in the middle" between top management expectations and the feelings and performance of front-line workers /people in your department.

First-line Managers (Shift Managers, Crew Leader, Third Key): Focus on the day-to-day workflow and problems. Often, they are the ones dealing with customers, keeping everyone on track, record keeping, and reporting, balancing cash drawers and making deposits at the bank.

If you are not already aware, think about managers you've had or positions you've held, and decide which category they fall into. Often there is a lot more happening around us at work than we even realize! It is not uncommon for management positions to be a mix of these categories or a combination of all of them in very small businesses.

Chapter 19
What Does A Leader Look Like?
Views on Leadership

Have you seen the movie Braveheart? Think about (or quickly search on YouTube), some of the famous speeches in that movie. Braveheart is powerful because it speaks to core values inside all of humanity: the fight for freedom, defending your family legacy, and the story of a common person rising to lead. The portrayal of William Wallace in that movie is an excellent example of how the Western world's subconscious views leadership: powerful, unquestioning, and commanding an army of followers. What movies like Braveheart and so many other American action movies focus on are singular leaders who give powerful messages and make excellent decisions under life-threatening pressure.

    While I also love inspiring leader stories, that is not what a real business leader typically looks like. They typically wear more clothes than Mel Gibson did and often do less public speaking/screaming. Tragically, some potentially great leaders end up *not* leading because they don't feel like they fit the bill.

Over the last 60 years, there have been so many theories and classifications in the study of leadership. The interest in studying leadership has seemed to dramatically increase over the last 20 years, most likely because it is a big money maker. There *are* certain things that make leaders great. Some people are born with those elements, and some have to work at it. Make no mistake, all great leaders have had to develop their skills, and many would look back on their past and see things they regret.

The Great Man

The oldest understanding of leadership, **The Great Man Theory**, viewed leaders as a unique type of person: you are either born a leader, or you just don't have what it takes. This understanding would say that successful leaders have an "it" factor, and if you don't have that unique essence, you will never be a great leader.

This sentiment has been passed along through the ages, and many have bought into this idea. Humanity tends to idolize and elevate certain people we admire, far beyond what we should. Before social media, cell phone cameras, and instant transfer of information via the internet, leaders were people the common person did not have access to. We would hear powerful speeches or hear *about* them, hear stories of the good that was done, and this passing along of un-vetted information became a type of hero lore that turned good leaders into icons. This background spurred The Great Man Theory. While this theory is comforting to our humanity because we all yearn for a trustworthy hero, it has proven itself to be wishful thinking at best.

These days, we see famous people's daily lives, hear about their divorces (and see related legal documents), can see all of their casual comments on social media over the years, and have seen many leaders taken down because of leaked recordings. It's evident that our leaders have flaws and are even bad people at times. The modern world has made us skeptical of those in leadership, and probably rightly so.

Trait Theory

Along the same train of thought of the Great Man Theory, researchers began studying what traits all great leaders had in common. This led to the development of **Trait Theory**. You are intelligent enough to recognize that ideas do not live in a box, so it's not surprising that this interest in "traits" eventually spread to other areas of study. These concepts have been used to create personality profiles, worker assessments, and leadership training.

Not all lists of traits that have come out are equally valid (one list had "being male" as a trait many years ago). The list of traits that have stood the test of time and scrutiny are objectively true and more agreed upon by everyone. There are many and several combinations, but some of the central leadership traits that are universally accepted today are things like: intelligence, creativity, decisiveness, trustworthiness, and emotional intelligence.

This theory led to the development of commonly used tools today, such as the Myers-Briggs Type Indicator (the assessment that determines if you are introverted or extroverted, among other traits), the 16PF Questionnaire, and the Five Factor Model. If you apply for a job and they have you take a personality test or a questionnaire asking about personal habits and how others see you, often they are looking to see what traits you possess. Traits are used today by many businesses and managers to determine whether a person is a good fit for a position.

Self-Reflection: do you feel like it is fair or appropriate to try to figure out a person's personality traits before fully considering them for a job? Do you think assessments can truly determine a person's personality and character?

Transformational Leadership

Some of the other approaches to assessing what a good leader looks like have focused less on what a leader possesses within themselves and more on how a leader behaves or impacts others. **Transformational Leadership** is an approach that identifies leaders who lead through change or difficult circumstances, bringing about positive results, along with their followers having gained internal benefits as well. They are dynamic leaders who make difficult decisions, show strong character, and pull the group together to achieve more than they thought they could. Again, this isn't about the leader's intrinsic qualities, but more about their impact on the group they lead through action and unifying.

One example of a transformational leader was Captain "Sully" Sullenberger, who did an emergency landing of a commercial airplane on New York's Hudson River. Not only did he demonstrate excellent skill as a pilot, but he also led his crew and passengers to safety in a number of ways. In a business context, leaders like Jeff Bezos are sometimes considered transformational because they revolutionized the way the consumers behave, and the way we do business. The list goes on, but distinct features make these leaders transformational both for their followers and the businesses they lead. A leader is usually only considered transformational *after* they have done something transformational – not before.

Notable Transformational Leaders: Nelson Mandela, Jeff Bezos (Amazon), Reed Hastings (Netflix), Oprah Winfrey, Capt. Chesley "Sully" Sullenberger (Flight 1549)

Authentic Leadership

Authentic Leadership is an approach to leadership I personally try to emulate. These types of leaders try to be transparent about who they are and what they stand for (virtues, morals, values), seeking balance in their decisions (seeking equity), living virtuously, and have genuine communication. Authentic leaders are people who are not afraid to show their humanity because they recognize that it is not a person's perfection that makes them a leader, but their ability to lead in an honorable way. Authentic leaders have a tone of humility, which is a key component missing in many leadership books and courses. They are also defined by leading with equity, empathy, courage, and authenticity in their communication. People tend to want to follow authentic leaders because of their air of trustworthiness and honesty.

Notable Authentic Leaders: Martin Luther King Jr., Billy Graham, Abraham Lincoln, Warren Buffet, Bill Gates

Servant Leadership

The leadership approach that has had some of the most profound impact on my personal life is **Servant Leadership**. This often-misunderstood approach sees the leadership role as a sacred honor and puts the group's needs above their needs. After landscaping, my first job was at Chick-fil-A, a fast service restaurant, and I will never forget the example of Doug Pugh, the restaurant owner.

Doug hired based on character and your connection to their mission of being positive, friendly, and family-based. He liked hiring family members, friends, and people who had good reputations because "good people know other good people." This approach worked because everyone I worked with were just really great people. What I will never forget is how he worked alongside us all. He wore a tie and dress pants but would cook fries, wash dishes, clean the floors, help and greet customers, and run register. He was not "above" cleaning the bathroom or taking out the trash to the dumpster. He didn't say things like, "I've been where you are – keep working, and you can be like me." What he said with his action was, "No one is too good for any job at this store – we're in this together." After a while, I almost wanted him to go to his office and leave the grunt work to us because I didn't want him to have to get in the trenches. That is servant leadership. Their humility and dedication to the cause makes you want to humble yourself and work harder.

In the first century AD, Jesus of Nazareth taught that if someone wanted to be important or lead, that they should put themselves last and commit to serve.[11] Taking his own advice, he got on his knees and washed his disciples' feet (an act of servanthood at the time), setting an example of humility for leaders instead of expecting others to bow to his needs. It doesn't mean leaders can't lead or do their specific tasks. It is an attitude of the heart while leading where they are also setting an example with their actions. Think of the impact of seeing the CEO of a large corporation getting on their knees to fix a toilet or answering the phones for their assistant so they can take care of a personal emergency. Servant leadership is revolutionary.

Notable Servant Leaders: Gandhi, Jesus of Nazareth, Mother Teresa

Few leadership approaches can touch the impact of Authentic and Servant Leadership because it gives those who follow a clear picture of who you are inside. A leader who is above everything is inspiring. A leader that feels nothing is beneath them creates loyalty and devotion.

The reality is that a "good leader" can look a million different ways. If you feel that you lack in an area or don't have the traits you wish you had, you can change. You can work on yourself. Different industries, organizations, and social scenarios call for different types of leaders too. Not all leaders are suitable for every situation. Leadership is not a "one size fits all" role. We desperately need people with different gifts, personalities, and visions to step up. Will you be next?

Think About It: Do you possess any leadership traits mentioned above? If you are lacking, how do you suppose you can grow in these areas?

Chapter 20
I Have the Power!

Do you remember being a kid? Do you remember who you wanted to be like? I was surrounded by the stories of powerful heroes who took matters into their own hands and took care of business - Superman, Luke Skywalker, G.I. Joe, Optimus Prime, and He-Man. I quickly found out that I was not equipped to solve the world's problems quite like they did. A cursory analysis of my heroes will show that each of them had different types of power. Superman was an alien, Luke was a kid who tapped into the Force, G.I. Joe were members of an elite military group, Optimus Prime was a big robot alien, and He-Man...was probably really into protein shakes and CrossFit...but gained strength "by the power of Greyskull"...so like, magic or whatever.

    Different types of power have been identified by some smart people over the years. As I will mention in my chapter, "How to Get Rich QUICK," you cannot just pass along power to people – it is something you gain over time, through an event or experience, training, or something you are born into. Let's look at the main types and see: 1. what power you have access to, 2. what power you may want more of, and 3. what power others have over you!

Different types of Power:

1. **Legitimate**: Power given to you by holding an official position such as becoming the president of your organization or a supervisor.
2. **Coercive:** Getting people to do what you want by force or through the threat of punishment ("Do this, or I'll break your legs").
3. **Expert:** When you are the best at something, people intrinsically trust what you say on the topic (Elon Musk or Warren Buffett).
4. **Referent:** Power gained through personality and influence. This would be like "the coolest guy in school," who has power through relationships.
5. **Reward:** The ability to reward someone via status, gifts, or another method. This would be someone very wealthy, famous, or even a hiring manager at Amazon.

Breaking down the types of power might seem arbitrary at first glance, but it helps to be able to define why someone holds authority or why you may take issue with how a leader is wielding their position.

Legitimate Power is a helpful distinction because it explains why someone might be dense, but they are somehow in charge. When a person is granted a position and is given a title, it doesn't matter if they are qualified for the position – it matters that they *have* it. Anyone who is elected to be in the White

House, for instance, will have legitimate authority to make decisions that affect the entire world, regardless of their qualifications. That is why being an educated voter matters. Holding the position of President, Vice President, etc., automatically gives you political, social, and pretty much all types of power.

There is an age-old question that asks if someone is a good leader, and then measuring their leadership ability by the loyalty of their followers. There are famous leaders like Abraham Lincoln, who led with ethics and dignity, and people followed due to his legitimate power, and arguably his referent and expert power as well. Then there are infamous leaders like Hitler, who also had quite the following, but he led by exerting far more than legitimate power. He also arguably had referent power, but more explicit was his coercive power. This element is vital.

When discussing this topic, it is helpful to differentiate between being a "good" (meaning moral or virtuous) and being an "effective" leader (meaning they get a job done). Hitler was effective, but he was effective *because* if you resisted, you were imprisoned or killed. Lincoln was effective, but he was effective *because* his message and character were worth following. They both used their charisma and inspiration, but what you inspire people towards will define your *goodness*.

When leaders motivate out of fear, coercion ("do this or else"), or through manipulative tactics, they may get results, but they will not get true loyalty. I've seen many managers and leaders think they are doing well because people do what they say, but no one respects them. The minute something better comes along, those followers are out of there. You do not want to be that type of leader. You want people to follow you because they want to and because they believe in where you are taking them.

There is nothing wrong with having boundaries as a leader and expecting high performance from your team. Setting expectations and keeping people accountable is completely appropriate, but some people confuse a parent's role with the role of a work supervisor.

As a parent, it may be appropriate at times to use some coercion and an expectation of unquestioning obedience, but as a supervisor, these dynamics are not the same. Yes, you can yell at your kids, and they will still love you…but your supervisor won't be tucking you in at night (let's hope not!) like your mom will. There is an extra layer of relationship that supervisors don't have. As a leader, it is your responsibility to use your power in a healthy way.

I once had a manager who treated me like her kid; I think because I was the same age as her 20-something year old kids. She would get in these moods, and snap at me, and then want affirmation from me. I would come in, and she would be grumpy, and then tell me to go clean the store so she could "be alone for a bit." She would want to hear about my day, and it would feel like she "wanted to know how school went" (I was in college at the time). Then something would happen, and she was suddenly this high-powered fashion designer with very distinct social graces. I got the feeling that her style of management was "I manage people all the time; I raised two children!" It's not the same – or rather, should I say it *shouldn't* look the same. Do not manage adults like you manage your children, no matter how old they are. That level of relational intimacy and drama is inappropriate to put on employees. There needs to be a separation between personal and professional interaction. A good manager gets things done through clear expectations, appropriate motivation, and mature communication.

So, again, an employee/employer relationship has power dynamics, but they need to be appropriate. The role of a supervisor is to make a team efficient and effective. You create loyalty through rewards, not just threats of punishment. Build respect by being trustworthy and consistent. The power balance in this relationship is a careful blend of various elements.

Moving away from thinking about power that impacts your work, there are other types of power in your life. Expert power is when someone has authority based on their knowledge and experience in a certain field. We should listen and give special attention when an "infectious disease expert" speaks on a particular virus. If the FBI says that something is being investigated, we should feel secure knowing they are very effective at investigation.

I often notice how we sometimes misattribute power and authority based on a title. Have you ever seen a news show where they bring in an expert, but they are not an expert in the field they are discussing? If someone has the pre-fix "Dr." before their name, that doesn't mean they are an expert on all topics. If a person has a doctorate degree, they have the title "Doctor," and what that means is they have over 20 years of education and are an expert in their specific field. There are medical, surgical, and healthcare-related doctors, and then there are people with doctorates in psychology, sociology, business, literature, and theology. Just because someone is an expert in one field, doesn't mean they are an expert in all fields – though they may have some other areas of expertise.

When you are in school or some other social situation, and there is someone who walks in, and everyone turns their head to watch them come in – that is Referent Power. This type of power is gained through being attractive, wealthy, cool, fun, adventurous, amazing at sports, or some other socially based feature. There is an aspect of envy and reverence with Referent Power.

If you are the richest kid in school or the richest person in your circle of friends, people may want to be around you based on your Reward Power, meaning your ability to buy or give certain unique gifts. Maybe they could get someone a good job, or be invited to eat expensive food, use cool gadgets, or even ride in an expensive car. This is the dynamic that many celebrities talk about when they say it is hard to tell if the people around them actually are friends or if they just want something from you. People with a lot of reward power may often wonder about the motivation of others.

Chapter 21
Yeah, I Know
Confidence

It is commonly believed that the number one thing your fellow humans pick up on when they identify someone as "attractive" or "sexy" is confidence. Confidence doesn't just mean being the frat guy with his hat on backward, crushing a can on his head, proclaiming he is "the king" of something or other. That guy might have confidence, but that would be better defined as a confident lack of self-awareness. Think about confident people you know. Confidence is self-assurance and the ability to trust your own decisions and encouraging others to do the same. Confidence is king. Confidence will take you places.

Have you ever seen movies or tv shows about "con men"? People will say, "They got caught up in a con and lost a lot of money," and talk about how some swindler convinced them to give them something (usually money or possessions) that they shouldn't have. A "con man" is short for "confidence man." The mere existence of such a profession speaks to how important confidence is to everyone. As Abraham Lincoln once said, "If you say something confidently, everyone will believe you!"

Abraham Lincoln didn't say that, but saying it confidently made you believe me for a second, didn't it?

Imagine a young man asking a girl out on a date that he has only previously said "hi" to a few times. He has no confidence, and looks down at the floor a lot, and is constantly fidgeting with his shirt. If he walks up to her, stammering and talking in circles about "You know, going out...with me...in public...and we can eat food", but never quite lands the proposition. She isn't likely to be a believer that this guy is going to fulfill his promises (or suggestions?) and has very little to go on. Not liking their odds, some girls might just say no thanks, while other girls might agree out of pity. None of those girls are going to be expecting much.

Now, imagine the same guy with confidence. Same look, same everything, but with his head held high, and his body and demeanor is calm. He is steady and comfortable in his own skin and clothes. He doesn't have to be more physically fit or classically handsome. He walks up to the same girl calmly, and intentionally, says she is the most beautiful and interesting girl he has seen. He asks if she would be interested in going out for dinner sometime, followed by a light-hearted movie and that she is welcome to bring a friend if it makes her more comfortable. He says he wants to have a fun night out, and he would gladly pay for her and her friend if she were interested.

Any awkward "cold call" date invite is going to be uncomfortable - but which guy would you feel more confident will actually show you a nice time? The second one, of course. He described a perfect evening, answering hesitations up front, and seemed to think of everything - his assurance would be more intriguing to the average person. Confidence is attractive and makes the person on the other end believe you will do what you say you will do. This is true in all areas of life: job interviews, presentations, performances, etc.

Ironically, confidence doesn't mean you are *able* to do what you say you will do. The unconfident guy might have been a millionaire, and the confident guy might not have a penny to his name...but he is most likely to get the opportunity. Just like in the professional world, often it's the candidates with the most confidence that get jobs in interviews. That doesn't mean that person is the best candidate; it means they are the best at *projecting that they are*. If you show full confidence in what you say, people naturally assume you know what you're talking about, even if you have no clue.

Are you a confident person? Are there areas of your life where you feel you could do better?

I wish I naturally had more confidence when I needed it. I have plenty of self-confidence when I am in certain circumstances, but I struggle in other cases.

I know the pain of not getting a job because I spoke like I wasn't intelligent or did not project the right vibe. Now, I do my best to mentally get in the game and visualize myself in that position. I try to train my thought processes in the direction of the job duties and the appropriate authority level. I do my best to smile, shake their hand confidently, and speak with appropriate but 'higher than average' energy. I try to project confidence and a calm demeanor, showing this job is not too much for me or beneath me - I'm just right for it.

As you lead and gain the trust of those around you, remember that confidence is key. It's not everything - but it can be the difference between getting an opportunity or not.

Chapter 22
Hey Bro, Are We Good??
Ethics

"What is Truth?" - Pontius Pilate, Roman governor, 33 AD

You cannot take everyone's advice. In fact, there is some standard advice that could get you in a lot of trouble. "Looking out for number one" naturally will alienate those you love because putting yourself first is self-centered. If you "follow your heart" instead of following the law of the land, you may end up in jail!

    I give a lot of tips and advice in this book, but you are the only one who can truly dictate how you live your life at the end of the day. In fact, some of the most significant decisions you make in life will never be vocalized to someone else – you will make them instinctively, or it might feel too personal to talk to someone about. Our lives are made up of millions of decisions that we make based on our conscience and our value system. We have daily opportunities to cheat, be honest, connect, reject, accept, or go all in. These decisions might lead to who you choose as a spouse, what type of career you choose, turning down a lucrative opportunity, saying something controversial at work, or possibly even doing something illegal.

Values, Morals, Ethics, and Legality are essential concepts to understand in your personal and professional life. We need to understand how and why we make the important decisions that we do. I won't say all that could be said, but this will at least get you thinking. Please note that even though I have my own strong opinions, values, morals, and ethics, I will define and discuss these topics in the most basic sense. You don't have to agree with everything said here, and you may be uncomfortable with other people having the freedom to live or believe a certain way. This is the real world, though, and our world is vast - not everyone thinks or lives as you do – but we all have to deal with our own values, morals, ethics, and legal expectations.

Values are your core beliefs and opinions about the world. These are always rooted in your cultural background, religion or lack thereof, family background, and personal experience. Values are opinions based on perspective, which should *not* be forced on others. Examples: "Education is important for success"; "Men should be the head of the home"; "My parents are Democrats, and I am a Democrat." Often, values are not stated out loud in public, but they govern how people live their lives.

Moral/Immoral: This is your definition of whether an act is "right" or "wrong," usually in keeping with a certain set of personal principles. Morals may be based on your religion, your deeply held cultural or family values, or the law of the land in your state/country. Some might even say they don't believe in morals and everyone has the right to make their own choices...but even the most progressive/liberal individual will draw the line at rape, murder, and theft. They will usually say that someone else's choices are none of their business, as long as something is "not harming others,"...which is a value. That value of "not harming others" dictates a "right" and "wrong" scenario...so, therefore, that is a moral. While morals are things we often hold to the strongest, we also need to recognize that our morals are based on our values, personal religion, or identification with a particular body of laws. Examples: "Adultery is wrong"; "You should always tell the truth"; "We should take care of homeless people." Some virtuous and principled people need to be reminded that unless something is breaking an actual law, that we can only share our *opinions* as to what we believe is "right" or "wrong." It doesn't mean your morals are "incorrect," but it is also virtuous to respect the views of others and to allow them to have their own worldview.

Legal / Illegal: Legality is directly tied to laws. If an act would break the law, it is considered illegal. Laws are universal and enforced by police officers within the stated jurisdiction. Examples: Stealing from a business is illegal in any country; waiting until you are 21 to drink alcohol is obeying the law in the U.S. This one is the easiest to understand.

Ethical / Unethical: Ethics are values, beliefs, guidelines, and practices intended to help a person maintain right standing. If the speed limit is the law, then ethics are like speed bumps – they keep you from breaking the law, but in of themselves, ethics are only legally binding in certain circumstances. Though, in healthcare, mental health counseling, the education system, and certain areas of business, there are ethical laws you must abide by to maintain your license and right standing in your job. Breaking ethical rules can *become* illegal activity, but they are not often illegal by default. Ethics are bound by the context. Sometimes ethics are required to be adhered to, and sometimes ethics are guiding principles that can be flexible.

For instance, it would usually be considered unethical for a manager to date an employee they are supervising since it could lead to compromising business practices. Dating, in this case, would not be illegal. If nothing is explicitly stated in the employee handbook about supervisors dating their subordinates, then it's technically allowable. Other employees may view the scenario as unethical, but they could still date if there are no official guidelines. On the other side, if a professional counselor started dating a client, this would violate counselor ethics, and they would lose their license to practice counseling. In some cases, a client could attempt to press legal charges against their counselor, claiming coercion and abuse of power. While it would be unethical, it would still be legal – but a lawsuit could lead to certain legal ramifications.

While all four areas may overlap (Values, Morals, Ethics, Legality), each topic is unique in itself. An action can be legal, but unethical. An action can also be legal, ethical, but immoral. If something is illegal, though, it is likely unethical, against some values, and immoral. Are you still with me? I know this is a lot.

If someone says they believe murder, stealing, and lying are wrong – those would be considered morals. Even if those things were legal, a person's morals and values could still say those things are wrong because their values might say all people should be treated with dignity and respect. Ethics, on the other hand, are more about adhering to standards of 'good practice' that emphasize fairness and equity among everyone involved. Often times, ethics are spoken about in more of a business or professional context. If a person in accounting approves payments that they know are not legitimate, it would be considered unethical.

Legality is based on whether something follows the law of the land. Morality is about following a specific set of values and can tend to be the most stringent and specific. Ethics tend to be a bridge between these two topics but is independent of the two – the focus is on whether something is fair, equitable, and how close something is to being illegal.

If you commit adultery / cheat on your spouse, that

would be considered immoral but legal. The ethics of that situation would completely be bound by context. If a psychologist cheats on his wife with a client, this would be considered immoral by most people, unethical by all people, but it is not an illegal act. When President Bill Clinton had an affair, it became a legal topic only because he lied about it under oath.

Forgive this illustration, but it is too perfect not to use. I do not go to strip clubs because I am married, and I am faithful to my wife, even in what I choose to expose myself to (*morals*). I also do not support that type of business because the whole system preys on struggles and desires that often lead to unethical and illegal behaviors (attributing a negative view of the system shows my *values*). These clubs have a *legal* right to operate, though, regardless of how I feel. The only *ethical* conflicts would be for me *personally*, since I believe they are harmful to dancers and patrons, or if going would lead me to lie about it.

The strip club could be an ethical business. If they checked the dancers and patrons' IDs, enforced the appropriate legal behaviors, including minors not purchasing alcohol - that would mean they are ethical in how they do business. It would be both a legal and ethical business; not only following laws but verifying, as a rule, shows the use of ethics. If they do appropriate background checks to ensure all the dancers are over 18 years of age, they are acting *ethically*. In the real world, there are often big issues with strip clubs and ethics. The general concern is that many do not do appropriate age verification on dancers, and there is a lot of "looking the other way" when it comes to what happens in private rooms. To add another layer to the system, if a club chooses to ignore what happens in private rooms, they may cross into prostitution, which is *illegal*.

Here is something more practical. Let's say your organization required you to have the customer sign a form to confirm that a job was completed before a bill was sent. We'll call it "Form C." An ethical dilemma would be if you were put under a lot of pressure to get your Form C signed by the customer so the company could be paid, but the customer wouldn't sign it. The customer refusing to sign is ultimately going to penalize you. If your supervisor puts tons of pressure on you, you may feel tempted to be unethical and forge a signature. You know the work is done, so what would the harm be? The ethical thing to do would be to take the penalty and wait for a valid signature. Forging a customer's signature on a form is wrong and could lead to other legal issues down the line if you are caught. This issue is genuinely about ethics. Supervisors need to be careful about how they pressure or penalize their employees to not give unspoken permission to make unethical decisions.

How We Make Decisions

My personal opinion is that even if you don't have specific morals or an organized religion that you follow, it is important to stand for something at least. I've heard too many people bristle at the idea that they should have any absolutes, but it's not a good idea to live your life that way. We all have certain values that we abide by, though we may not be consistent in our behaviors. If you don't have a set of morals or values that you follow, it is easy to make compromises over the course of your life that could lead to other problems and pain you were not wanting.

If you have a 'live and let live' attitude about your marriage, you are not protecting each other. If you are not protecting each other, you are leaving an opportunity for things to happen that could deeply wound your spouse and thus ultimately end in divorce. If you do not want a divorce, it is important to find personal standards that you abide by at least to show value and respect for your spouse. Using the previous example, if an affair would be a deep violation of trust in your marriage that would lead to divorce, then it would follow that you maintain boundaries for yourselves that keep each other from getting too close to that line. This would be an example of personal ethics.

Action Point: Take a moment and write down four of your personal values (deeply held beliefs about the world). Then write down four morals (right/wrong) based on those values or similar. Finally, write down four ethical principles you follow based on your other principles (principles that keep you from taking immoral or illegal action).

A Wad of Cash in an Envelope

In a lot of textbooks and ethics classes, they may say something like, "No one is going to offer you an envelope of cash for you to do them a favor, but..." I wish that were true because I definitely have been offered that.

I was in my mid-20s while working as a youth director in an immigrant community in Chicago. For about 20 reasons, I will keep this vague, but this is an example most people couldn't give. I found myself intervening on behalf of a youth in my group, and their parents were involved. I drew a line in the sand with the youth's immigrant parents and basically told them if they do something again that was considered illegal and putting their child at risk, I will call the police. I wasn't trying to threaten, but I was drawing a line in the sand and making sure they understood their level of accountability. Apologies and assurances were made that they would make things right.

The next day, I walked into my place of employment and was met with my supervisor, who was in charge of the organization. He frantically took my hands and placed an envelope of cash in them. It was about 4 inches thick with hundred-dollar bills spilling out, no exaggeration. I don't know how many thousands of dollars were in there, but it was easily a couple months of my wages. I was dirt poor, this was my job, and this was my boss. He said, "No police, James. They are good people. No police."

I was very culturally insensitive by loudly asking if I was being bribed and almost throwing the money back. I felt deeply grieved that someone in authority would pass along a literal bribe to me, expecting that to satisfy my desire for the protection of a young person in my care. In the two years following, I never heard a word about any further issues with that family, which was a relief.

My values in this situation were that I was doing this job for the good of these youth and the community and that I had a much larger purpose than just doing a job. I needed the money more than you can imagine, but my morals would say that taking a bribe and betraying the trust of a young person I was supposed to protect was very wrong. Any ethical measure would determine this as a major violation. I later realized that if something ever went south with that scenario, I could have been in legal trouble as well. *What would you do in this situation?*

There are situations where bribes would be considered *cultural expressions of gratitude or respect* and not as an affront to ethics and morality. As a businessperson, non-profit leader, or just a regular person, you should never accept cash or large gifts of any kind "under the table" or outside of an agreed upon legitimate payment. You can reject it gracefully, but reject it, nonetheless. Plenty of people have gotten in serious trouble by accepting bribes or gifts that could be considered bribes.

This is why it is important to stand for something. If you do not have a value system, you are susceptible to making unethical decisions. Once you accept a "gift" of this kind, you are caught in a web of power play. Accepting bribes or expensive gifts will make you legally responsible if you end up in court. If you remain on the outside of that web, you maintain the power in the situation.

Yes, while you may not be handed an envelope of cash, being asked to look the other way…you might, though. Sometimes ethical dilemmas are apparent (and thus less tempting), and sometimes they are subtle. From a *legal* perspective, *subtlety does not matter*. So, stay alert.

Chapter 23
How to Get Rich QUICK!

Have you ever wondered about how many people have read "Get rich by following these simple steps" books and then got rich? There are a significant amount of books and YouTube channels dedicated to some dude driving a Bentley, with a white suit, slicked-back hair, touting bogus "secrets to becoming rich" (here's another secret: you're probably not going to get rich reading their books or by paying thousands for their seminars).

    Now, reading and educating yourself can help you, and at times can be the difference between failing or succeeding. A casual online search will show that a majority of millionaires are avid readers. Successful people think differently and usually are making educated decisions about the business choices they make, but they aren't reading books by the "get rich quick" people. A quick internet search will give you plenty of suggested books by the people you respect, but a couple favorites of Bill Gates and Warren Buffett are "Business Adventures", "Security Analysis", and "Stress Test." Interestingly, one favorite book of entrepreneurs is "The Millionaire Next Door." It talks about how most millionaires live frugal lives, and the people buying all the expensive stuff usually don't have as much as you think.

I've known some very successful people in my life. They sometimes have shiny smiles and nice clothes, but they usually just look like regular humans and may not even have nice shoes (gasp!). That's reality. Rich people sometimes wear bright white tennis shoes or old boat shoes, and sometimes they drive regular cars. Have you ever seen how Bill Gates and Mark Zuckerberg dress? They dress like men their age and don't try to be super trendy – yet they are a couple of the most successful and wealthy men on the planet. Think about that.

I've also known plenty of people who are not successful at all. They dress super fancy, trendy, and drive very nice cars, yet they are in debt and barely keeping their lives together. A friend of mine was in college, going to school for fashion design, and found a way to use student loans to pay for his BMW. He still lived at home and didn't have much of a job, but he wanted to look the part. Beware of people who look like they are *trying* because they just might be pretending.

I'm very skeptical of someone with a shiny suit and a big smile who wants to make sure you know the type of vehicle or plane they have - telling the rest of the world, "you can have all this too!" That's not how the world works. Not everyone can have all of that, honestly. There are people who have done everything and given everything to be wealthy and still aren't. As I discuss in this book, the slick, wealthy authors are respected because of their specific type of power – Reward or Referent Power, but it's not transferrable. Sorry. Can you learn from them? Possibly. Should you keep buying their books until you get rich? For crying out loud, please don't. We can learn helpful principles from successful people but beware of those people who spend too much energy trying to "flex" or show how wealthy they are, saying you can have it too.

Pro-tip: Be skeptical of the promise of anything <u>valuable</u> in this world that you don't have to <u>work hard for</u>. Lasting relationships, careers, wealth, and possessions come with an appropriate (the amount you would expect) amount of work.

This is not to say that someone might land a big account, high-commission sale, or overnight success with their business, and suddenly they have a lot more money. It happens, but you can't manufacture overnight success. Any of these people will tell you that their overnight success came after an appropriate level of skill, hard work, and sacrifice at some or all levels.

Let me put this another way. If you are aware of the Hip-Hop music scene on any level, you should be able to name at least one artist who is talking about how much money they have...before they are even famous! That is what is called "fake it until you make it." When people want to show that they live the rich and famous lifestyle, but they don't actually have the money to afford it...they can *rent it*. There is an industry where businesses rent luxurious cars, boats, homes, and clothes –

whether you are pretending for a weekend or are actually wealthy and just in town for a trip.

The "success game" is not all that you are being fed through social media, YouTube channels, and self-help books. Western culture has been brainwashed about success and what it looks like. We have been told that if you are rich, powerful, and famous, then you have it all, and there is a never ending well of cash for you. That is simply not true.

Many wealthy people who live extravagantly have had serious money problems: 50 Cent, Kanye West, and Donald Trump are three examples of people who have had cash flow issues even though they have made hundreds of millions over the years. Did you know that a lot of lottery winners have bankrupt a few years after winning? To maintain wealth, you need to manage it just like anyone else! You have to either continue working or find concrete ways to make your money multiply through financial planning. You can't retain your wealth if you spend extravagantly and don't have equal incoming funds. The wealthiest people in the world don't spend time trying to convince anyone about what's in their bank account. It should send up red flags when someone goes out of their way to tell you how ridiculously wealthy they are.

Back on earth…if we choose to learn proven business and financial management principles, apply them to our lives, and let those principles shape us - then over time, we can become the people we want to be. If you want to gain success and wealth, you need some education and to apply an appropriate level of skill, hard work, and sacrifice. Money should not be your only measure for success, but I know it helps you feel settled and happy when you can pay all of your bills.

Chapter 24
A Special Warning for Leaders
Triad of Danger

The last twenty years have taught us that leaders and powerful people sometimes have dark things to hide. Everything from the corporate scandals of the early 2000s to the issues related to the #MeToo Movement of the 2010s has exposed corporate greed, ignoring of ethics, sexual assault/abuse, abuse of power, and a litany of other evils perpetuated by people in positions of power and influence.

Looking at this from another angle, I have noticed incredible ignorance coming from articles and editorials that seem to not understand *how* anyone could ever do *anything* wrong in leadership. Not that "criminals need to be treated better," but more that there seems to be a misunderstanding of how some of these things are *able* to happen. If you are in leadership or aspire to be a leader, you *need* to understand *how* these scandals have happened so many times and by so many people. You also need to understand these things so you can protect yourself and others from the same mistakes.

This topic is a big deal and should not be taken lightly by anyone. Please know that my heart goes out to you if a leader has hurt you in any way, and nothing I ever say is intended to undermine anyone's pain.

Positions of Power and Influence

Let me start with some altruisms that are generally...uh, true.

1. Absolute power corrupts absolutely

2. Leaders struggle with: Money, Sex, and Power

3. With great power comes [equal] responsibility

All of these statements are true in their own way. Whether you are in an official leadership position, you have a position of influence (which equals power), or you are very wealthy (which also equals power), you have an extra level of responsibility to manage. You do not have to have an impressive salary or home to possess this. Some examples are managers, teachers, unpaid or paid organizational leaders, CEO's and VP's, doctors, famous entertainers, famous anything, religious leaders, and a host of others. I want to be clear that if any of those titles describe you, you need to hear that *you* are dangerous: to yourself and to others.

For the sake of redundancy, let's abbreviate Positions of Power (typically abbreviated as POP) and Positions of Influence

(POi) as **POPi***. I feel like the acronym looks weird, but it will keep us all from reading "positions of power and influence" too many times.*

Let's be clear: **If people <u>have</u> to listen to you, then what you say matters and what you imply to them matters.** (Let that sink in for a minute.) If you are in a POPi, then even your "off the stage" or "outside of your office" comments have weight. Things you casually mention or simple favors you may ask will feel weightier for that person than you might intend.

All POPi make the people they are over naturally vulnerable. We are often naturally attracted (in various ways) to people in POPi and, at minimum, feel like we want to please them (for various reasons). Whenever a leader allows someone to open themselves up in an inappropriate or any type of vulnerable way, it is *your* responsibility to protect them and yourself. Many people in POPi choose to be ignorant of this because it is an inconvenience at best. You can choose to be ignorant, but thousands of lawsuits have been filed in the last few years where a person in a POPi says an activity (any activity) was "consensual" while the other person disagrees – usually because they felt like they couldn't say "no." The person in the POPi might be someone they greatly respect, admire, or depend on in some way. This could apply to a work expectation, doing a casual "favor," romantic advances, disclosing personal information, or taking advantage of their vulnerability in any number of situations. The mini-series, The Morning Show, actually does a great job depicting these dynamics.

These principles apply to you even if you have low self-esteem or are very humble. Something I was blind to in my early adult life was that even if *I* don't feel like *I* have power in a scenario or if I feel insecure about myself, if the situation above fits you – it applies to you.

A simple example would be when my wife and I were out on a rare evening date, and her boss called. They said they needed her to come into the office to do something that was, from our perspective, unimportant. She clearly stated that we were out on a date and even had a babysitter – her boss ignored the details and asked when she could drop by. In most normal circumstances, a person might not give in to a friend, but my wife was vulnerable because she cared a lot about being a good employee and was already nervous about job security. She felt obligated to come in even though it hurt her heart and ruined our night. Whether her boss realized it or not, they were not protecting her as an employee. A simple favor is weightier than you would think.

The Ferguson Triad of Danger

The rest of this chapter will focus on the Ferguson Triad of Danger (a tongue-in-cheek title - just because I can), which is the "how" in *how* leaders can make the types of mistakes and unethical choices that they do.

People in POPi need to be aware of their own Opportunity, Greed, and Pressure. *It is your <u>responsibility</u> to* *manage these three areas just as much as you manage your own job responsibilities.*

Opportunity

People who aren't leaders and have never had influence usually have no idea what it is like "on top." The more power and influence you have, the more Opportunity you have to be irresponsible or to be tempted to misuse your power.

If you have never been responsible for depositing, managing, or using money for an organization, you have not had the financial opportunities that those in POPi have. Having *access* automatically allows you the opportunity to be trustworthy or untrustworthy in ways other people don't have. It goes without saying, but financial responsibility is a sacred trust. Having freedom in your responsibilities as it relates to finances automatically puts you at risk of misuse.

A cliché example of the disparity in a POPi's opportunity is if you were a famous musician. An accountant might look at this musician who is caught having an affair and think, "I would never do that." The accountant knows like ten girls, and three of them he is related to, while the musician has throngs of girls throwing themselves at him. The musician has a lot of opportunities, whether he is feeling emotionally strong or very weak. Who knows how the accountant would respond if given the exact same opportunity. When you are in a POPi, the opportunities are unique.

Greed

Our POPi also opens us up to the dangers of Greed. Greed is the thing inside us that says, "I still want more," even when we have enough. One might be so greedy in their heart that they would have to think very hard about whether something is a "need" or a "want." It can show up in many areas, such as in our relationships, work, money, possessions, and a lack of generosity.

The phrase "corporate greed" is what typically comes to mind when speaking of leadership and greed. In the corporate world, it is most pronounced in special financial perks for top management and in how hard managers push their employees with little to no reward. The subordinate employees are doing the bulk of the essential work, but those on top reap the most benefit. In all organizations, managers are paid more, and as I said previously, that is valid. They deserve to make more because they are responsible for more and the job performance of others. When managers do their job well, the impact of that one person (manager) becomes exponential, enhancing the work of the many under them. The misuse comes when top managers push everyone very hard, but the ones on top are the only ones who benefit – through things like profit sharing, bonuses, etc. In the last decade, the incredible wage gap between essential front-line workers who may earn $60,000 and under vs. those in VP and CEO positions who make millions has come to light, bringing extra attention to this salary inequity.

Along similar lines, have you ever worked in a position with high sales or performance goals? Once you met those goals, were there a lot of high fives and rewards? Probably not. Upon meeting that goal, we often immediately hear things like "Awesome. This is the new goal." I once worked for a department manager who regularly did this and touted "No one reads yesterday's newspaper. Let's look forward." You know, it's true…no one reads newspapers anymore. Though *I do* read yesterday's news because of the way my Facebook and CNN feeds work. Anyway. I know what he meant, but is it too much to let your employees feel good about themselves, celebrate, or offer some type of 'thank you'? That is incredibly demotivating. It's demotivating because someone is gaining profits, but it's not "me." People under our POPi feel our monthly pressured demands, but end up feeling like a hamster on a wheel – there is no end or reward in sight.

If you ever find yourself at the top of the corporate chain of command, remember that pressure compounds as it goes down. Those under you feel the pressure, so they pressure those under them, on down the line until the people at the very bottom feel incredible pressure. They might not even know why – and they surely are not being compensated for this performance. Those at the top, though, typically are. Greed blinds. The fatter you get with those profits and benefits, the more blind you become to the plight of those you have pressured to receive your profits. I guess its kind of like…corporate type 2 diabetes (eating too much leads to disease, and the disease can lead to blindness. That was probably a dad joke.). Aaaanywho.

Pressure

People in POPi typically are under a lot of pressure: to succeed, to look a certain way, to increase success, to hold things together, and bearing the burdens of a business. This pressure often leads to behaviors that are not great: drug abuse, finding solace in illicit relationships, gambling, over-spending, and over-eating.

It is important to find healthy ways to deal with your pressure. Driven people are often laser focused on what they have to do and want to do, that they are not paying attention to their own needs. When a person has opportunities, pressures, and power that other people don't have, they feel isolated and resort to self-regulating or self-soothing activities that are unhealthy but help them feel better quickly in the moment. We have to find healthy ways to manage our *pressure*. We also need to be aware of our own *greed* and recognize the unique *opportunities* we have been entrusted with.

Chapter 25
What You Do…Is Not Who You Are
Conclusion

So, who are you? Answer that question for yourself. I'll wait a minute.

Often times when we introduce ourselves, we start with our career, our titles, our education, and occasionally something personal. The truth is that we are complex beings, and the whole of who you are cannot be summed up in a sentence. You are shortchanging yourself if you try to define yourself by one thing.

First, we are often shaped deeply by our faith, value system, and cultural backgrounds. Second, we are defined by our relationships – for better or worse: you are someone's child, you are someone's spouse, you are someone's parent, you are someone's relative, and hopefully, at least one person would call you a friend. Thirdly, our personalities are made up of things like being outgoing, shy, pensive, bubbly, fun-loving, analytical, or someone who loves to "experience," and the list goes on. Lastly, we all have things we love and enjoy doing. We have hobbies, interests, recreation activities, and ways to recharge.

Our careers can also be part of who we are. While 'what

we do' can define an aspect of us and take up most of our time, it shouldn't *define us*. Our career can highlight all kinds of things about us — but what about when we lose our job or career? What happens when things are *not* going well at work?

I've found that when things aren't going well at work — it can color how I see myself and my personal value. The reality is that while that may matter on a certain level, I can still be a success as a husband, father, and son even if I'm unemployed. We need to make sure while we invest in our careers, that we also invest in our personal lives and the relationships around us because there may be moments in your life where that is all you have. That happened to me, and it rocked my world.

The converse of this is exemplified in former Apple CEO, Steve Jobs. When faced with his own mortality, he hired a biographer to follow him around so that his kids could know why he was gone so much and what his life was like. He spent so much time at work that he realized his own family did not truly know him. While Steve Jobs had a profound impact on the world through his work, that is not how I would like to feel at the end of my life.

Life is a balancing act. One minute we are solely focused on our career, school, a new relationship, a new baby, the next workday, or our next vacation - and at any one of those points, we will feel pulled back towards another part of our lives. In life, there is always competition for your attention and your energy.

May you find that balance and give your whole heart to

those who matter most to you. May you find joy in your life and experience it to its fullest. May you also find satisfaction and purpose in your work…and may it be your own personal WorkTopia.

The End

...or is it just the beginning?

*(Cue Music: *Dum, Dum, Dahhh!*)*

NOTES

Chapter 1: Work, Work, Work, Work, Work
1. Rene Descartes, "Discourse on the Method of Rightly", Conducting the Reason, and Seeking Truth in the Sciences, 1637
2. Plato, Allegory of the Cave, 517 BC
3. The Holy Bible, Genesis 2:15
4. "Work". The Oxford Online Dictionary, 2020

Chapter 4: Hey Laptop, What'cha Doing This Friday?
5. Theodore Roosevelt famously wrote to his friend William Bigelow, March 29, 2898 "Comparison is the thief of joy"

Chapter 5: Slow and Steady Gets a Raise?
6. Michael Jordan in the Nike Commercial titled "Failure"

Chapter 6: Know Thyself
7. Plato, The Apology of Socrates, 399 BC
8. Quote attributed to Aristotle

Chapter 7: Are We Done Yet? No, Never
9. Andy Stanley, When Work & Family Collide. Multnomah Books, 2011 - formerly published as *Choosing to Cheat*

SECTION II: Navigating Today's Job Market
Chapter 10: My Corporate Ladder is Broken
10. Adam Davison, The Passion Economy. Vintage Publishing, 2019

SECTION III: Rising to the Top
Chapter 19: What Does a Leader Look Like?
11. The Holy Bible, Mark 9:35

About the Author

James Ferguson lives in Ohio with his wife, their four children, two cats, and a turtle. James teaches business and leadership courses at Kent State University and also works for a Fortune 500 company as a project manager. He has a bachelor's degree focusing on non-profit leadership, a Master's in Organizational Leadership, and is currently working on a Doctorate in Business Management. In his spare time, he enjoys listening to and playing music, being a nerd about Star Wars and music history, and having deep conversations over coffee or buffalo wings. He is a treasure-trove of useless pop culture information and previously taught about ancient literature and history for fifteen years.

WorkTopia.info / contact@worktopia.info

www.ingramcontent.com/pod-product-compliance
Lightning Source LLC
Chambersburg PA
CBHW052355220526
45465CB00003BA/1113